# Teaching Media Ethics

## Master Class
### Resources for Teaching Mass Communication
Series Editor: Chris Roush (University of North Carolina–Chapel Hill)

*Master Class: Teaching Advice for Journalism and Mass Communication Instructors,* by the AEJMC Elected Standing Committee on Teaching, edited by Chris Roush

*Testing Tolerance: Addressing Controversy in the Journalism and Mass Communication Classroom,* by the AEJMC Commission on the Status of Women, edited by Candi Carter Olson and Tracy Everbach

*The Graduate Student Guidebook: From Orientation to Tenure Track,* by the AEJMC Board of Directors, edited by Katherine A. Foss

*Teaching Race: Struggles, Strategies, and Scholarship for the Mass Communication Classroom,* by The AEJMC Minorities and Communication Division, edited by George L. Daniels and Robin Blom

*Teaching Media Ethics: Integrating Ethics Across the Mass Communication Curriculum,* by The AEJMC Media Ethics Division, edited by Nicole Kraft and Kathleen Bartzen Culver

About AEJMC
The Association for Education in Journalism and Mass Communication (AEJMC) is a nonprofit organization of more than 3,700 educators, students, and practitioners from around the globe. Founded in 1912 by Willard Grosvenor Bleyer, the first president (1912–1913) of the American Association of Teachers of Journalism, as it was then known, AEJMC is the oldest and largest alliance of journalism and mass communication educators and administrators at the college level. AEJMC's mission is to promote the highest possible standards for journalism and mass communication education, to encourage the widest possible range of communication research, to encourage the implementation of a multicultural society in the classroom and curriculum, and to defend and maintain freedom of communication in an effort to achieve better professional practice, a better informed public, and wider human understanding.

About the Series Editor
Chris Roush served as the dean of the School of Communications at Quinnipiac University. In 2010, he was named Journalism Teacher of the Year by the Scripps Howard Foundation and the Association for Education in Journalism and Mass Communication. The judges noted that Roush "has become the expert in business journalism—not just at Chapel Hill, but throughout the country and even in other parts of the world." He has also been named the North Carolina Professor of the Year by the Carnegie Foundation for the Advancement of Teaching and Council for Advancement and Support of Education.

# Teaching Media Ethics

## Integrating Ethics Across the Mass Communication Curriculum

The AEJMC Media Ethics Division

Edited by
Nicole Kraft and Kathleen Bartzen Culver

ROWMAN & LITTLEFIELD
*Lanham • Boulder • New York • London*

Published by Rowman & Littlefield
An imprint of The Rowman & Littlefield Publishing Group, Inc.
4501 Forbes Boulevard, Suite 200, Lanham, Maryland 20706
www.rowman.com

86-90 Paul Street, London EC2A 4NE

Copyright © 2024 by The Rowman & Littlefield Publishing Group, Inc.

*All rights reserved.* No part of this book may be reproduced in any form or by any electronic or mechanical means, including information storage and retrieval systems, without written permission from the publisher, except by a reviewer who may quote passages in a review.

British Library Cataloguing in Publication Information Available

**Library of Congress Cataloging-in-Publication Data**

Names: Association for Education in Journalism and Mass Communication. Media Ethics Division, author. | Kraft, Nicole, editor. | Culver, Kathleen Bartzen, editor.
Title: Teaching media ethics : integrating ethics across the mass communication curriculum / by the AEJMC Media Ethics Division ; edited by Nicole Kraft and Kathleen Bartzen Culver.
Description: Lanham : Rowman & Littlefield, 2024. | Series: Master class : resources for teaching mass communication | Includes bibliographical references and index. | Summary: "Filled with classroom-tested strategies to integrate ethics into all media courses, this book is an essential resource for all mass communication instructors. Part of the AEJMC Master Class series, the book gathers expert authors to share decades of teaching experience to help teachers prepare students for ethical media careers"— Provided by publisher.
Identifiers: LCCN 2023036321 (print) | LCCN 2023036322 (ebook) | ISBN 9781538183069 (cloth) | ISBN 9781538183076 (paperback) | ISBN 9781538183083 (ebook)
Subjects: LCSH: Mass media—Moral and ethical aspects. | Mass media—Study and teaching. | Ethics—Study and teaching. | Journalistic ethics—Study and teaching.
Classification: LCC P94 .A79 2024  (print) | LCC P94  (ebook) | DDC 302.23071--dc23/eng/20230819
LC record available at https://lccn.loc.gov/2023036321
LC ebook record available at https://lccn.loc.gov/2023036322

# Contents

| | | |
|---|---|---|
| Introduction | | vii |
| 1 | Media Ethics Defined<br>*Patrick Lee Plaisance, Penn State University* | 1 |

**Part I: Ethics at Every Level**

| | | |
|---|---|---|
| 2 | Undergraduate Media Ethics: An Introduction<br>*Patrick Lee Plaisance, Penn State University* | 11 |
| 3 | Teaching Advanced Undergraduate Media Ethics<br>*Patrick R. Johnson, Marquette University* | 19 |
| 4 | Graduate Seminars in Media Ethics<br>*Ryan J. Thomas, Washington State University* | 27 |
| 5 | Diversifying the Ethics Curriculum<br>*Chad Painter, University of Dayton* | 37 |
| 6 | Inclusive Teaching as Ethical Practice<br>*Patrick R. Johnson, Marquette University* | 45 |

**Part II: Ethics in Every Area of Study**

| | | |
|---|---|---|
| 7 | Developing a Combined Media Law and Ethics Course<br>*Jack Breslin, Iona University* | 55 |
| 8 | Ethics in Introductory Reporting Courses<br>*Lee Wilkins, University of Missouri and Wayne State University* | 65 |
| 9 | Ethics in Photography and Visuals<br>*Alex Scott, University of Iowa* | 73 |

10  Public Relations Ethics Education in Advanced Courses        83
    *Katie R. Place, Quinnipiac University, and
    Xiaochen Angela Zhang, University of Oklahoma*

11  Ethics in Broadcast News Classes                              91
    *April Newton, Loyola University Maryland*

12  Ethics in Student Media                                       99
    *Nicole Kraft, The Ohio State University*

## Part III: Ethics in Specialized Topics

13  Covering Law and Justice                                     109
    *Kathleen Bartzen Culver, University of Wisconsin–Madison*

14  Data Ethics                                                  113
    *Jasmine E. McNealy, University of Florida*

15  Sports Reporting                                             119
    *Nicole Kraft, The Ohio State University*

16  Digital Ethics                                               123
    *Julianne H. Newton, University of Oregon*

17  Relational Journalism                                        129
    *Paul S. Voakes, Paula Lynn Ellis, and
    Lori Bergen, University of Colorado*

18  Covering Mental Health, Suicide, and Substance Use           135
    *Kathleen Bartzen Culver, University of Wisconsin–Madison*

19  Social Media                                                 139
    *Sheila B. Lalwani, University of Texas at Austin*

20  Science, Health, and Environmental Journalism                143
    *Rhema Zlaten, Colorado Mesa University*

21  Foreign Correspondence                                       149
    *Sheila B. Lalwani, University of Texas at Austin*

## Part IV: Ethics Beyond the Classroom

22  Teaching the Ethics of Civic Journalism                      157
    *Mark Poepsel, Southern Illinois University–Edwardsville*

23  Media Ethics is for Everyone                                 167
    *Joseph Jones, West Virginia University*

Index                                                            175

About the Contributors                                           183

# Introduction

> Ethics is knowing the difference between what you have a right to do and what is right to do.
>
> —Potter Stewart, Supreme Court Justice of the United States, 1964, *Jacobellis v. Ohio*

To be an instructor of communication practice or theory is to teach ethics.

Words have power, and those of us who wield words in any form across media have a responsibility to do so ethically to ensure those we communicate to, for, and about are treated with the respect they deserve.

It is with that mandate in mind that the Media Ethics Division created this book in collaboration with AEJMC.

Some who teach in the media and communication fields believe ethics are best handled by other instructors—those tasked with the classes that contain ethics in the name. But it is impossible to teach reporting without providing the ethical filters that guide interviewing, reporting, writing, and publishing. Classes in public relations must recognize framing and messaging ethics.

Ethics help us frame the concepts of right and wrong, and guide human behavior and decision-making. Ethics give us a framework to ask what is just or virtuous, as well as understand the consequences of our actions. Ethics shape the relationship between ourselves and the obligations we have toward others, toward society, and toward the world.

The thread of ethics connecting all of communication is a guiding principle on which the majority of skills will be developed. It allows students to navigate complex questions, identify and foster respectful dialogue, and contribute to a more socially conscious society. Among the key elements framed by ethics are truthfulness, accuracy, and transparency. Ethics hinder the proliferation of disinformation, manipulation, and deception.

Digital media presents its own unique challenges and opportunities, both of which require an understanding of ethics. Integrating ethics into communication classes provides students with the critical thinking skills necessary to navigate challenges in media production, journalism, advertising, and social media. It also provides students with a framework for ethical decision-making in various communication contexts, through the use of theories, principles, and models.

While many facets of media industries make use of ethics codes that are informative and guiding, they provide principles, as opposed to an actual framework for teaching others to behave and work ethically. There are also numerous wonderful books on ethics for students to learn from and explore specific cases, many of them written by the extraordinary authors we have gathered here.

Despite these resources, AEJMC recognized there is often no real opportunity for many faculty to learn the *teaching* of ethics. Many are simply provided a syllabus and told an ethics class is now their responsibility. Even more are steered toward other communication or media classes without any understanding of how to build ethics into the foundation.

That is where this book comes along.

We have gathered together some of the foremost authors, researchers, educators, and advocates working in media ethics to teach current and future teachers to incorporate the field in all aspects of communication coursework. A glance through the table of contents is truly a who's who of the finest ethical minds—members of the Media Ethics Division. Among our many contributors are faculty from across the academic landscape, teaching journalism, multimedia, communication, public relations, advertising, and more. They include authors of noted ethical texts and research, including:

> Lee Wilkins, professor emerita from the School of Journalism at the University of Missouri, is coauthor of *Media Ethics: Issues and Cases*; *Entertaining Ethics: Lessons in Media Ethics from Popular Culture*; and *The Moral Media: How Journalists Reason About Ethics*; and a founding editorial board member of the *Journal of Media Ethics*. She writes on ethics in introductory reporting classes.
>
> Patrick Lee Plaisance, the Don W. Davis Professor in Ethics at the Bellisario College of Communications at Penn State University, serves as editor of the *Journal of Media Ethics* and authored *Media Ethics:*

*Key Principles for Responsible Practice*, and *Virtue in Media: The Moral Psychology of Excellence in News and Public Relations*. He writes here on defining media ethics and teaching it to undergraduates.

Ryan J. Thomas of Washington State University, the director of graduate studies in the Edward R. Murrow College of Communication, has been published in such journals as the *Journal of Media Ethics, Journalism Studies*, and *Digital Journalism*, and writes on graduate seminars in media ethics.

Chad Painter, University of Dayton's department chair of communication and coauthor of *Media Ethics: Issues and Cases* and *Entertaining Ethics: Lessons in Media Ethics from Popular Culture*, writes on diversifying the ethics curriculum.

Collaborating on relational journalism is the trio of Paul S. Voakes, Paula Lynn Ellis, and Lori Bergen, coauthors of *News for US: Citizen-Centered Journalism*. Voakes is professor emeritus at the College of Media, Communication and Information at the University of Colorado Boulder and coauthor of *The American Journalist in the 21st Century* and *Working with Numbers and Statistics*. Ellis spent 26 years with Knight Ridder and serves as a senior associate at the Kettering Foundation and a trustee of the Poynter Institute. Bergen, founding dean of the College of Media, Communication and Information at the University of Colorado Boulder, is coauthor of *Media Violence and Aggression: Science and Ideology*

The importance of ethics in communication classes cannot be overstated. Integrating ethics into the media curriculum means students are better equipped with the skills and knowledge necessary to engage in responsible, honest, and respectful communication. As media continue to shape our personal and professional lives, teaching an ethical foundation ensures our graduates uphold the values to foster a healthy democracy. We are grateful to everyone who is willing to tackle this extraordinary and important teaching role, and hope this book helps you.

*Nicole Kraft and Kathleen Bartzen Culver*
*Editors*

# 1

# Media Ethics Defined

Patrick Lee Plaisance, Penn State University

How might news editors justify publishing, or withholding, images of death and destruction from a natural disaster? What does it mean to say an Instagram influencer should behave "responsibly?" What moral obligations might television entertainment producers and documentary filmmakers have to audiences and to the idea of "truth?" What does "professionalism" look like for a public relations executive whose ideas don't align with those of a client?

These are the sorts of issues and questions that move us into the realm of media ethics.

They call on us to draw upon and consider normative claims from moral philosophy (of which the philosophy of ethics is a branch) and articulate why an act/decision/behavior is morally justified in the production or use of media content. In doing so, we employ moral assertions about the nature of goodness, harm, and other concepts that rest on the work of philosophers and theorists spanning more than two millennia. But we also are called on to move beyond mere assertions about goodness: the philosophy of ethics, properly understood, emphasizes the hard work of deciding what to do when no obvious "right" solution shows itself—when we must find a defensible way to prioritize two important "goods," or values, for example, when we find ourselves in a situation in which it may be impossible to promote both.

In journalism, dilemmas regularly arise from the clash between the important but often-conflicting duties of informing the public and minimizing harm (to someone's reputation, to their privacy, etc.). We can *assert* the importance of both in journalism all day long. Ethics, however, calls on us to think through what criteria we might use to prioritize one in certain situations. The philosophy of ethics is concerned more with the deliberative processes we use to find a defensible course of action and less on making moral assertions about the nature of goodness (which is the focus of moral philosophy).

## WHAT IS MEDIA?

The question may seem banal, but it is worth contemplating. It should be evident that the term *media ethics* comprises issues of judgment and morality across all media sectors—news, advertising, marketing, public relations, corporate communications, as well as social media platforms and the uses and effects of various media technologies. Media is a concept that is so broad and vague as to be nearly useless, and yet all of us can have very different schemas of meaning that are triggered by the term. For some, it's cable anchors Jake Tapper and Sean Hannity. For others, it's the *New York Times*. For still others, it's Disney+ and Amazon Prime Video. Or TikTok and Instagram. Or a favorite blogger. Or FM radio. Or an email newsletter. The point is that *media* is all of this. Depending on the image that the term evokes in our heads, we may link it to a host of very divergent ethical assumptions, such as:

- Free-speech constraints
- Content aimed at persuading
- Journalistic bias

The point is that the vagueness of the term likely means that we may all start at very different places in our media ethics conversations, and with very different assumptions, knowledge levels, and expectations. Our digital (and highly fragmented) media environment further complicates the picture, as we are unlikely to have a widely shared media experience online. Most Americans have low levels of news literacy and often don't understand what distinguishes journalism from other kinds of narratives they see. They may not distinguish between reporting and commentary, for example. Many users are only dimly aware of the thorough convergence in our digital world: Yes, the *Wall Street Journal* is also on social media; social sites can be news content creators; companies regularly publish their own "stories" through sophisticated branded content.

This confusion and disconnection poses significant challenges for understanding media ethics. As we will discuss, many key principles and standards apply across media sectors. Honesty, transparency, and respect all matter, regardless of whether communication channels are being used to inform audiences, persuade listeners, or sell a brand. But some ethical claims can be mistakenly applied based on what kind of "media" content we are talking about. It makes little sense to apply journalistic standards of balance and impartiality, for example, to advertising or promotional messaging—or to the commentary of pundits found on cable news programming, for that matter. Precision in what we mean by "media" is critical for any effective ethical deliberation. Some work in the field has leaned on the term while limiting itself in fact to a focus on one area, such as journalism ethics. Scholars can often devote their attention exclusively to a single media sector (e.g., public relations ethics) in valuable ways, but to use the *media ethics* umbrella term while doing so risks misleading audiences.

## WHAT ARE ETHICS?

As stated earlier, ethics refers to the claims we make about goodness, how things *should* be (normative claims), and how we can best bring those claims to bear in our deliberations about finding the best course of action in dilemmas that require us to manage conflicting values. Such a definition should make clear that ethics are not a single formulation or frame of thought. We certainly can talk about a single ethic, such as the ethic of justice, or having a good work ethic. Doing so emphasizes a focus of concern in an area of life or work. The universe of *metaethics*, however, is much broader, encompassing multiple, and often competing, frameworks proposed to guide behavior and decision-making. Metaethics is concerned with how we know what we refer to as "moral facts," and how our moral claims inform our lives. It explores connection values, reasons for action, and human motivation, and it addresses many issues commonly bound up with the nature of our freedom and our moral responsibilities.

Take, for example, the "value" of beneficence (which Aristotelian theorists would call a virtue). We can see the idea discussed and manifested in social welfare programs, scholarships for the needy, philanthropy, policies to protect animals, admissions policies, disaster relief, and many other areas. In metaethics, we would ask such questions as:

- What makes these things beneficent?
- Are such beneficent acts and policies required of us all?
- Do they merely represent the pursuit of optional moral ideals?

Most ethicists also remind us that it is important to recognize the difference between *moral assertion* and *ethical deliberation*. The first simply invokes a claim about goodness or rightness that is presumed to be true: *It is always wrong for a journalist to lie to a source.* Moral philosophers through the ages have been deeply concerned about how exactly we *know* something to be good or bad. What exactly are we saying when we make such judgments or assertions? Are we grasping some intrinsic reality about the thing in question, or are we just presuming that our intuitions and emotional responses are true? Most of us don't tend to spend time questioning the "goodness" of things; we often just presume that to be self-evident. For casual conversation, that serves us well enough. But ethical deliberation calls for thinking carefully in cases where two or more "good" things or values are in conflict. We understand that journalists shouldn't lie to sources, because their very existence is premised on the premium placed on truth-seeking. Lying as a means may not justify the end, and doing so can seriously undermine their credibility. But what about when letting bad actors know you are a journalist would prevent you from uncovering a major story of wrongdoing and, thus, undermine your ability to carry out your journalistic duty to inform the public? The ethical dilemma posed by this scenario requires us to move beyond merely asserting that all lying is bad, and to consider an argument that will justify prioritizing one of the values (informing the public) over another one (not lying).

Within the philosophy of ethics, we also see a distinction between *theoretical* ethics and *applied* ethics. Theoretical ethics generally focuses on big ideas about goodness and abstract conceptualizations of principles such as what constitutes a duty—or, again using the example of beneficence, how we might want to place limits on its scope to accommodate other interests when making decisions or policies. Applied ethics focuses on more concrete situations or applications of concepts, say in a professional setting. For example, what is the proper role of beneficence in biomedical or business ethics? Media ethics, too, is generally considered a type of applied ethics. The same principles or values may be important in different ways in different settings, such as autonomous agency, harm minimization (or nonmaleficence), and transparency. For example, transparency is often a primary issue in media ethics, since being aboveboard and enabling audiences to make their own judgments about content is central to professional credibility. But such transparency may be less of a concern in, say, engineering ethics.

## METAETHICS FRAMEWORKS

Most media ethics courses on the university level emphasize an applied-ethics approach, and rightly so. A major goal is to get aspiring media professionals to understand what it means to do a job well and responsibly. But a curriculum that is not sufficiently grounded in theoretical ethics risks becoming just a series of talks about best practices, and such a course fails in helping students reach another, equally important goal: to get good at responding to difficult ethical dilemmas with solid ethical reasoning skills. They will not have the necessary tools to do so if they remain unfamiliar with theoretical ethics. A good media ethics course will provide a grounding in the various metaethics frameworks, so that students understand the importance of moving beyond gut-level responses and relying on mere moral assertions that might seem useful only in contexts in which other people with similar beliefs will agree with them. These metaethics frameworks help students get good at ethical deliberation and make more sophisticated ethics-based arguments. They help students think deeply about the nature of virtue (courage, for example) or what it means to be virtuous; about the concept of duty and how to understand our moral obligations to act in certain ways and not others; and how to negotiate conflicting interests conscientiously.

Through the ages, philosophers of all stripes have provided and debated various ways to think through ethical dilemmas. Here is a brief list of some of the more common frameworks:

## Virtue Ethics

Developed initially from the work of Socrates and Plato, and later expanded upon by Aristotle, virtue ethics emphasizes the reasons we have to develop good character and to learn how proper understanding of virtues should shape our behavior. Only through deliberate contemplation of virtues (charity, courage, temperance, patience, etc.) and a focus on continually aspiring toward conditions of human flourishing (eudaimonia) do we achieve *phronesis*, or the practical wisdom needed to live our best lives. All this takes time and effort, however, and the enterprise is fraught with complications. These include our pleasure-seeking natures, the role of emotions in contemplation of virtue, the need for (and, often, the scarcity of) exemplars from which we can learn, and the reality of conflict in communities. Aristotelian thinking and virtue ethics fell out of favor until St. Augustine's writings in the first century, and it was again largely dismissed in moral philosophy until advocated by Elizabeth Anscombe in a landmark essay in 1958. Since then, virtue ethics has enjoyed a revival of sorts, reflected in the work of philosophers such as Anscombe, Alasdair MacIntyre, Rosalind Hursthouse, and Philippa Foot.

## Duty Ethics

Theories of deontology, or duty ethics, argue that we have objective reasons to honor a set of obligations we all have as moral agents in the world.

The question asked in duty ethics does not involve one's character but whether one's intent aligns with our moral duty. If so, any consequences that may result from that act are not morally relevant. As moral agents, we are all bound by certain duties that transcend personal preference, social norms, or culture, such as the duty to tell the truth, keep promises, respect others, and avoid causing harm. One of the most influential proponents of duty ethics was German eighteenth-century Enlightenment philosopher Immanuel Kant, who argued that moral duties are based on a rational and universal principle he called the "categorical imperative." This principle requires individuals to act only in ways that they could to become a universal law, and to always treat others as ends in themselves rather than as means to an end. Kant argued that since our capacity for reason and our free will constitute the core of our humanness, these two features deserve special respect in everything we do. Kant provides an inexorable system of logic as the basis for morality, yet his work tends to frame moral duty in rather monolithic terms. Other duty ethicists, however, have offered more refined efforts that recognize the reality that our moral duties, such as the ones referred to earlier, often conflict. More useful is to consider how to articulate moral reasons for prioritizing one duty over another in a given situation. W. D. Ross is one philosopher who attempts this, arguing that we have several "prima facie" duties that can supersede each other depending on situational factors.

**Consequentialist Ethics**

As the label suggests, this approach places the moral weight of a question on the outcome or result of a decision rather than on one's character or intent. Among the most predominant of these approaches is John Stuart Mill's utilitarianism. The rightness of a decision is defined by its *utility*: how effective it is in mobilizing or ensuring resources to bring about the most good for the greatest number of people. Maximizing happiness, Mill said, refers not just to hedonic pleasure but also to things such as general welfare, appreciation for culture, and justice. Since the work of Mill and, before him, Jeremy Bentham in the eighteenth century, utilitarianism has been a cornerstone of many political systems. However, it is not the only consequentialist framework; many offer different approaches to take outcomes into account. Some emphasize potential harms that might result in a decision. Others reject Mill's majoritarian focus. One of these is the "distributive justice" theory of John Rawls. For Rawls, who argued that utility failed to adequately account for a range of moral concerns (such as inequality and persecution of minorities). He proposes a novel thought experiment involving what he terms the "veil of ignorance" that promotes decision-making premised on maximizing liberty and yet also protecting society's most vulnerable or most disadvantaged.

These three approaches—virtue, duty, consequence—historically have dominated Western philosophy of ethics. But there are still other approaches:

**Ethics of Care**

This framework rejects the priority that others place on abstract concepts such as justice, or disembodied notions of duty or wisdom. Instead, it centers ethics in the reality of our social lives, and at the center of our social lives is relationships. Care ethics has been developed and promoted since the 1980s by feminist and environmental theorists and emphasizes that moral significance is found in our dependency on other people and the situational features we find ourselves in with others in our lives.

**Communitarianism**

Whereas most Western thought prioritizes individual rights as the key criteria for many political and moral questions, communitarian theorists suggest doing so wrongly minimizes the primary role that community belonging plays in the shaping of individual identity. Community values and concerns, they say, must have a prominent role in our moral decision-making. This collectivist approach is found in many Asian and African cultures; one example is the Zulu concept of *ubuntu*, which roughly translated, means, "I am, through others."

**Confucianism**

Often perceived as analogous to the virtue ethics of Aristotle, Confucian ethics emphasizes living in ways that embody respect, social cohesion, and self-improvement. We emulate elders and leaders for their ethical leadership, and we must value hierarchical order. Much as Aristotle says that cultivating virtuous habits is how we attain *phronesis*, or practical wisdom, Confucius wrote how our goal should be the cultivation of *ren*, or benevolent goodness, in all we do.

**Feminist Standpoint Epistemology**

Whose voices count? What groups have historically been silenced? Whose experiences matter? By asking these sorts of rhetorical questions, feminist scholars have highlighted the gendered nature of power and argued that both knowledge and authority is shaped by social power and disenfranchisement. They document how the voices and perspectives of women have been systematically silenced or oppressed, and they argue that due to their experiences, women can provide critical insights into our shared reality, and even perhaps uncover truths that patriarchal systems may have obscured.

Notice that some of these are overlapping in nature. Others offer diametrically opposed systems of deliberation, such that applying them to the same ethical dilemma may well result in different responses. This is part of what is so unique about the subject of ethics—and why it can create so much frustration among students. As this listing of ethics frameworks demonstrates, the focus of ethics is not the final decision one might make. In true ethical dilemmas, there is never a completely "right" or "wrong" course of action. Whatever one decides, people are likely to declare your decision unethical. Rather, the true focus of ethics is the quality of our deliberation that we can show supports what we see as the most defensible solution or response.

A solid media ethics curriculum, then, seeks to invite students to see ethics not as a discouraging search for nonexistent "right" answers but as training, for both our personal and professional selves, to become better at asking the right questions.

# I
# ETHICS AT EVERY LEVEL

# 2

# Undergraduate Media Ethics: An Introduction

Patrick Lee Plaisance, Penn State University

Of all the college curriculum levels, media ethics instruction is arguably the most challenging with less-experienced students. It aims to orient students on relatively sophisticated content—metaethics, the Socratic process, professional media situations often heavy with ambiguity and many moving parts—at a time when critical-thinking skills are still under development. It is also a challenge because of the likely chasm between the media experiences of the youngest college students and those of their instructors.

At this level, the best instructors are those eager to be "schooled" about the latest media habits, platform trends, and language patterns in an effort to close that gap. That chasm, however, also includes wide disparities in levels of media literacy: A regular "diet" of actual news and journalistic content is increasingly rare among the younger generations, so basic distinctions that may be critical in good ethical deliberation—between news and opinion, between journalism and promotional content—often requires emphasis. It is also valuable to spotlight research that documents the negative effects of our technology use on our media literacy. For example, people who rely exclusively on their social media feeds for news are most likely to exhibit low levels of political knowledge, and are most vulnerable to misinformation and fake news.

Much of the work of undergraduate media ethics instructors is simply aimed at ensuring that students start on the same page, with a common understanding of the roles of media sectors. There are several good-quality news aggregators that can facilitate this, such as Semafor. Setting regular expectations about news consumption and devoting class time to discussing news topics, as well as how news articles are constructed, can go a long way in boosting literacy and fostering curiosity about ethical challenges in media industries. Ultimately, media ethics and media literacy are deeply intertwined at the introductory level, and instructors must be willing, when possible, to spend as much time on one as the other. Students who don't understand the basic tenets of American journalism, for example, and haven't developed a news habit, are more likely to make ill-informed judgments about what journalists do and why. Productive deliberation on questions of media ethics requires a strong (or at least nominal) media literacy.

Yet for instructors who embrace this condition, undergraduate media ethics instruction can be among the most rewarding. It is the perfect time to emphasize the value of grappling with challenging "gray" zones, and to model resisting the impulse to find comfort in the oversimplification of issues into black and white. A key component of wisdom and intellectual maturity is the ability to deal effectively with ambiguity. This, of course, is related to a core concern of ethics, which is how to responsibly negotiate among conflicting values. The early college applied-ethics course is the perfect place to frame the difficulty of doing ethics as a source not only of frustration but of intrigue—even as a path to wisdom. It is not a bad thing that we are still talking and debating ethics millennia after Plato and Socrates. Rather, it suggests the endless fascination of the topic, and the constant relevance of questions about what constitutes a moral life.

## ETHICS THEORY

Instructors of introductory-level media ethics courses shouldn't presume their students have much, or any, exposure to philosophy. Such courses must find the delicate balance between keeping ethics theory accessible, yet at the same time indicating its depth and complexity. There are many media ethics texts available to help do this. Professional ethics codes are useful in helping students with media literacy and getting them oriented to standards and norms of media professionals. They also illustrate the distinctions between duty-based ethical statements (e.g., "Seek the truth and report it") and calls to be concerned about the consequences of our actions (e.g., "Minimize harm"). Introductory courses aren't likely to delve into deeper metaethical issues—the deontological differences between Immanuel Kant and W. D. Ross, for example, or a comparison of modern-day virtue ethicists. But they should provide a grounding in basic tenets of metaethics: that moral assertions are best avoided; that true ethical dilemmas are ones that provide no single "right" solution; that the quality of deliberation, rather than any final decision, is central.

Popular culture provides fun and useful entry into media ethics. Depictions of journalists in film and television provide reliable prompts for good ethics discussions. Examples are *Spotlight, Shock and Awe, The Insider,* and *Shattered Glass*. All four of these are based on real-life events—the *Boston Globe* investigation into sexual abuse by Catholic priests; the lone Knight-Ridder news bureau that questioned the weapons-of-mass-destruction rationale for the 2003 Iraq invasion; the CBS mishandling of a Big Tobacco whistleblower; and the destruction of the credibility of a national magazine by a prevaricating staff writer, respectively. All four raise critical questions of journalistic independence, corporate conflict of interest, and harm. Can't afford class time for full-length films? Carefully selected clips also can be valuable.

Other shows provide accessible ways to engage introductory-level students with ethics itself. The NBC hit sitcom *The Good Place*, starring Ted Danson and Kristen Bell, tells the story of the transformation of a demon (Danson) who becomes intrigued by the human concept of morality, and the show revolves explicitly around ethics—and stands as the only Hollywood production for which not one but two moral philosophy professors were hired as consultants on the set. (It doesn't hurt that one of the main characters is a moral philosophy professor who everyone loves to ridicule.) Entertaining yet educational show clips that provide comedic takes on the trolley problem and other moral questions can be found on YouTube. One of the hired philosophers, Todd May, also is featured in clips that discuss concepts such as utilitarianism and the categorical imperative in the lighthearted context of the show (also easily found on YouTube).

## CASE STUDIES

While upper-division media ethics curriculum may focus more heavily on abstract theory and ethics principles, case studies can be effective and engaging centerpieces of lesson plans. They simultaneously provide exposure to media practices (good and bad) and direct student focus to central ethical issues. The best use of case studies is a Socratic approach: beginning with questions or observations aimed at achieving a full understanding of relevant facts, followed by questions that spotlight the motivations of actors, the values reflected in decisions, and the effects on relevant stakeholders. While it may be tempting as instructors to offer our own judgments about what should have been done in a particular situation, the goal should be healthy discussion and consideration of possibilities.

In the case of all courses, but particularly applied ethics courses, instructors must work to ensure an environment in which all students feel risk-taking is OK and in which they are encouraged to participate in frank exchanges with their peers. More often than not, moments of epiphany occur when they are impressed by something a classmate says rather than by words from their instructor. Case studies are valuable both in fostering this kind of environment and in encouraging a healthy and respectful back-and-forth.

When using a case-study approach, instructors should choose cases carefully. The best cases are truly "gray" in nature—they offer scenarios in which there is no obvious "right" response, and in which the central values in conflict are both clear and apparently irreconcilable. They also have been carefully written and presented, and they provide thoughtful suggested questions to focus discussions. Several media professions—journalism, public relations—have associations that provide case studies, but well-curated archives may be more eclectic. Here are three such sources for case studies on issues from across media sectors:

- The Center for Media Engagement at Moody College of Communication at the University of Texas: https://mediaengagement.org/vertical/media-ethics/research/
- The Center for Journalism Ethics at the University of Wisconsin–Madison's School of Journalism and Mass Communication: https://ethics.journalism.wisc.edu/the-shadid-curriculum/
- The Markkula Center for Applied Ethics at Santa Clara University: https://www.scu.edu/ethics/focus-areas/journalism-and-media-ethics/resources/cases/

**PRINCIPLES**

At the intersection of metaethics theory and case studies lie relevant concepts, or principles, that help us frame ethical dilemmas, highlight what matters, and define what constitutes the most optimal or defensible course of action for a given situation. This chapter offers a small set of such principles, though there might be many others to explore. They connect with most every possible media ethics case study, but to get the most out of Socratic discussions of a specific case, it is important to get students grounded in these principles. Encouraging students to think deeply about them, and not simply acknowledge that they are important, can raise the floor of the discussion of a case.

## HARM

Look at most any ethics code, and you will see some expression of the need to be concerned about potential harm, or an admonition to avoid or minimize harm. The concept may seem straightforward, but it tends to get quite complicated very quickly the more it is considered. When should harm be avoided at all costs? There are many varieties and dimensions of harm: physical, psychological, reputational, financial, etc. How might we quantify harm? Many students may presume that if a case poses a significant likelihood that harm may occur, then that's the end of discussion, as nothing else matters. But in fact, concern for potential or even actual harm can be outweighed by other values. Acknowledging this can usher in more difficult yet valuable discussions about how, in some cases, harm may be inevitable, but that doesn't mean it can't be responsibly minimized in some way.

## AUTONOMY/RESPONSIBILITY

This duality poses a regular source of moral tension: the exercise of independence or autonomy versus honoring our obligations to others, which often implies some sort of constraint or limit on the former. Numerous philosophers have offered paths to delve deeply into the role and value of each in our lives. In Western societies, the culture of individualism tends to place a premium on freedom, which thus is used as a trump card, questioning the legitimacy of *any* limits on our autonomy. The concept of moral autonomy, however, is the idea of exercising our freedom while recognizing our obligations to others. Some theorists have described it as not the freedom to do as one pleases but the ability to take ownership of the reasons for our actions. Moral autonomy, then, can help reframe issues about freedom as, "What moral rules have I freely accepted as a moral agent," and "How might I use those rules to guide my decisions and behavior?"

## PRIVACY/COMMUNITY

Like the autonomy/responsibility duality, the tension between the need for privacy and the pull of community is a common feature of media ethics issues. Again, fruitful debates or discussions require attention to each concept to identify how they connect to our moral agency and flourishing. Doing so raises the odds of students moving beyond platitudes. Privacy is essential for all of us—to enable us to develop ourselves and to help us manage our various social roles. As important as it is to be able to remove ourselves from scrutiny, accountability also is important. Being held to account is a measure of respect. Privacy claims aimed at merely dodging accountability have less validity than claims that are clearly connected to the reasons we have to value privacy. Similarly, it is valuable to prompt students to think about the extent to which our identities are rooted in social ties and community belonging, and how so much of our moral agency is in fact determined by these motivations and connections.

**Transparency**

For media ethics, some degree or requirement of transparency is often fundamental to responsible practice. For professionals in media, it refers to conduct that presumes an openness in communication and serves a reasonable expectation of forthright exchange when message recipients or audiences have a legitimate stake in the possible outcomes or effects of the message. Transparency implies a concern that recipients be given all they need to exercise their own judgment and not be thwarted by deception or omission of important information, even when such obfuscation may be in the interest of the communicator. Cases involving questions of transparency center on when a lack of transparency—the use of hidden cameras by journalists, say—might be justified. What other significant values or interests might be furthered or promoted by a lack of transparency, and what is the impact on credibility?

## ASSIGNMENTS

There are many types of writing exercises that can augment media ethics class discussions. Carefully considered assignments can encourage students to grapple with ethical concepts and value conflicts rather than just spout a series of moral assertions or opinions.

- Short, informal "response" essays on a specific reading before a class discussion on the topic can "raise the floor" of the conversation, as students will more likely come having better-developed thoughts or questions.
- Assignments that call on students to pick a case study, discussed above, and craft an argument about the best solution using ethics theory are aimed at improving both students' critical thinking and ethical deliberation. These argument essays also can be paired with one of the many ethical reasoning tools available, which help students

focus on key ethical questions or issues and avoid getting sidetracked into commentary or interesting but ethically irrelevant information.
- A more demanding assignment type would be a media analysis, where students delve into extensive coverage of a news topic or public relations communication campaign, to consider themes or patterns of narrative, framing, and rhetoric that define the content. Such an analysis, and not a mere description of single stories, can enable students to consider ethical questions possibly raised by the content.

# 3

# Teaching Advanced Undergraduate Media Ethics

Patrick R. Johnson, Marquette University

Instructors can teach introductory ethics courses in several ways, each dependent on what prerequisites departments require. I took "Introduction to Ethics" in the philosophy department before enrolling in "Ethical Problems in Mass Communication." The requirement of an introductory ethics class allowed my instructor to focus on practical applications rather than theoretical constructs. The requirement was still in place when I taught that same course three years after taking it. The university later changed its core curriculum, and the College of Communication dropped the required ethics prerequisite. That change meant students were no longer required to have a foundational knowledge of ethical theory before entering my class, and I needed to shift how I taught the course and the texts used.

In surveying syllabi of journalism schools around the country, ethics courses can be found in all layers and levels of the curriculum. For example, one has a 1000-level course focusing on films, while another has a specialized upper-division, senior-level course on ethical branding. Introductions to philosophy are the most consistent, and few courses are taught without explicit normative theoretical grounding. Western theories are the most present in courses, with Eastern or feminist theories lacking inclusion. Course titles aren't consistent, focusing on communication studies, media, strategic communication, or journalism. Several include the term "diversity" in their title. Some instructors merged the ethics course with a media law course. Identifying that specialization in a course is one way to create an advanced ethics class.

Advanced media ethics can also be a rumination on metaethics, usually absent from introductory courses that favor questions of normative ethics.

Introductory ethics courses focus on practical ethics and provide spaces for students to address questions of right and wrong relative to media practices and behaviors. Positioning students in a place to move beyond the routine and contemplate how moral language or moral thought helps frame the field shifts the level of thinking from introductory to advanced. Utilizing metaethical questioning as a course focus provides a space to think about the interconnectedness of values and behaviors while also considering social and cultural implications that lead to what motivates us and our decision-making. I offer this approach with caution.

Ethics courses often rely on the moral reasoning of established, privileged voices. These voices are traditionally male and Western, despite Eastern and Global South representatives, females, and LGBTQ+ persons offering thoughtful critiques and questions. With such diversity in scope and sequence in course design, it is hard to pinpoint what approach would define an advanced media ethics course that wouldn't represent components of an introductory course or blend into a graduate-level seminar while considering diversity, equity, and inclusivity. Because of that, I suggest focusing advanced courses to give students experiences that build rigorous content knowledge while also developing personal resilience and an ethics toolbox.

## PROJECT-BASED LEARNING

Bridging theory and practice isn't the most straightforward task for students. Given the difficulty of the ideas we often explore, learn, and discuss, it could be even more difficult in our media ethics courses. In an advanced media ethics course, a way to create that bridge is by utilizing project-based learning (PBL). According to author and educator Michael McDowell, PBL "is an inquiry-based methodology that follows a distinct pathway of learning that organizes levels of rigor into a particular sequence."[1] In PBL, the teaching focus is on inquiry and is developed by providing students with real-world problems to solve or examples to deconstruct. Utilizing project-based learning in an advanced media ethics classroom is easy by following these steps:

- *Step 1:* Students are given a context to a problem or idea that stimulates thinking. Inquiry becomes the driving force of learning. This stimulant could be something introductory, like a video, or more contextual, like an argumentative podcast episode.
- *Step 2:* Students then design a plan to solve that problem by considering the course content and additional research (primary and secondary). This plan should acknowledge the role of the audience and how

it may be connected to the problem. A solution is a response to the audience's need.
- *Step 3:* Students work through the problem and take note of the critical thinking moves they need to make, problem-solving strategies they utilize, and different avenues to address the question.
- *Step 4:* Students present findings.
- *Step 5:* Students reflect on the process and share how they could solve the problem differently if they addressed it again. Students would also reflect on their strengths and weaknesses.

Reflecting on the process is essential, not just something students should do after the activity. The more attempts students make at project-based learning, the better the class and actions will become. After each effort, take notes on how you can refine the context or problem, provide more scaffolding for student success, or revise the assessment outcome to encourage more diverse student responses or outputs. The practice of PBL does not need to be unique to the topic of an advanced media ethics course. It provides an opportunity to elevate the content from an introductory course to an advanced level. Additionally, if the course is broader (meaning media ethics and not a specific topic), there are ample opportunities to diversify the project-based tasks to span media and disciplines.

*The Barbie Project.* One example is a project I used called The Barbie Project, in which I presented students with this problem: Barbie lacks diversity, and we must be responsive to evolving diversity, ethics, and inclusion (DEI) needs. I first did this project before Mattel attempted to diversify Barbie. Mattel's 2020 change led to modifying the activity to ensure students didn't recreate one of the executed changes. We began by reading Shirley Steinberg's essay "Barbie: The Bitch Still Has Everything." Through a close analysis of the piece, we dissected why Barbie had a diversity problem. In 2018, I could assign Hulu's *Tiny Shoulders: Rethinking Barbie* documentary. After students contextualized the problem, they began to plan out what this Barbie would be like—how they would respond to the problem. Students then developed production and marketing plans. They also wrote a report using research and philosophical theories about how their new Barbie responded to the problem. At the same time, students demonstrated how their Barbie reflected the audience they served. Students pitched the product to their class. We concluded with the group and individual reflections on solving the problem. Students would think about their inquiry process and discuss how and why ethical approaches to solving issues need to be responsive to the needs of communities. The reflections also helped students to identify what moral judgments help guide their behaviors and how differences in moral language or judgment can impact how we attempt to solve problems.

In addition to The Barbie Project, other options include using film to identify and address ethical values, examining nonfiction texts to process loyalties and theoretical problems, or creating podcasts to discuss ethics.

*Film Assignment.* For the film assignment, you can have students write a short analysis on a film appropriate or popular with young adults selected from a list (e.g., *Rebel Without a Cause*; *Clueless*; *Easy A*; *Love, Simon*; *Booksmart*). This would allow students to talk about representation in film. Students would need to look up and read the entry on the film on IMDb as well as film reviews from reputable news and entertainment sites. The film analysis should focus on how the film represents teenagers and their concerns and preoccupations by having students identify reasons the film appeals to an adolescent audience, as well as the messages the film conveys to young adult viewers. More specifically, students would focus on how adolescents are represented and what ethical concerns or values emerge in that representation. A film analysis could also be about the industry rather than representation. Students would choose a partner to evaluate a movie about journalism (e.g., *Absence of Malice, Spotlight, Capote, Almost Famous, Page One*). Each partnership will give a five- to seven-minute class presentation based on an ethical dilemma identified in the film. Students should provide key information related to the ethical dilemma and discuss how the dilemma was addressed in the film. In addition, they should draw on class lectures and discussions to help them evaluate how they would resolve the ethical dilemma, specifically focusing on values and loyalties. This same framework could also be accomplished using narrative nonfiction texts like *In Cold Blood, Missoula, The Voyeur's Motel*, or other examples. Podcasts are another contemporary example to which this form of analysis can be applied. When we think about these at an advanced level, here are several points you may want to address:

- An identification of the ethical dilemma;
- A thoughtful and thorough analysis of a possible role player who may face this dilemma;
- An identification of the key facts related to the dilemma;
- Use of outside research to understand the impact of the problems facing the role player;
- An analysis of the loyalties and values;
- An analysis of the most relevant ethical principle that will support making an ethical decision associated with the dilemma;
- An analysis of loyalties, counter values, and an ethical principle that will counter your ethical decision; and
- A thoughtful and concise ethical decision based on relevant loyalties, values, and principles you've identified.

Regardless of the assessment, PBL will guide the design to lead students through an inquiry-based approach to learning. Students move from traditional forms of knowledge, such as discussion or exams, to engaged educational practices.

## EXPERIENTIAL LEARNING

Experiential learning is like PBL, but students can see the inquiry in action instead of as insulated forms of inquiry. One of the most common examples of experiential learning includes student media, student-led agencies, and strategic communication campaign courses. Advanced ethics courses can borrow from those learning experiences by partnering with clients or newsrooms to solve ethics issues in their organization. It can also be an opportunity for students to engage with communities to address more significant questions of ethics and how media decisions and practices impact their daily lives.

According to the Experiential Learning Institute,[2] there are four steps in the "Experiential Learning Cycle":

- *Step 1: Experience.* This is the activity students participate in that allows them to think about what they are learning and how they are learning it.
- *Step 2: Reflect.* This step focuses on process and perspective. How do the systems lead to learning? Who is included in the experience?
- *Step 3: Think.* This leads students to conclusions about the experience and inquires about what they learned. It conceptualizes the experiences and helps contextualize the outcomes of the experience.
- *Step 4: Act.* This step is about implementation and, as the ELI states, "active experimentation or trying out what you learned." Students will return what they learned to the current experience or use it in future ventures, such as a job.

Experiential learning (EL) is a hands-on form that can cater to individual success. Participating in an EL activity also allows students to fail in a place where they can learn without extreme repercussions, such as being fired or sued. Experiential learning is similar to how Aristotle believed we know character and virtues: habits. Aristotle wrote, "We are by nature able to acquire them, and we are completed through habit . . . we acquire just as we acquire crafts, by having first activated them. For we learn a craft by producing the same product that we must produce when we have learned it."[3] The act of habitual practice is rooted in experiential learning. As a result, students who participate in it build up a toolbox of sharpened skills. In our role as instructor, we move from "sage on the stage" to knowledge facilitator. This transition means we can focus on helping students to engage critically in their individual learning experiences, cultivate life skills that can be transformed and translated to other experiences, and highlight opportunities for growth.

*Community Conversation.* A way to do this in an advanced ethics course could be by elevating research experiences to focus on community conversation and complicated dialogues. This activity requires students to work with communities they live in and those that may differ from their own. For example, they could gather a group of students like themselves or bring a more diverse group into the conversation. The students come to the table in search of an answer to a question of ethics and media, similar to a focus group. The students get to practice fundamental applied research skills while exploring topical issues in the media ethics course. Beyond this, ask students to write a code of ethics for a company. Students would interview employees and read company materials to understand the values and loyalties of the organization. When this happens, students can apply theoretical frameworks to create a functional code of ethics for the organization. Students can also do this for themselves. They can do self-interviews and think about who helped them learn the values they live by, how they came to understand them, and then which will help them live out an ethical future. Experiential learning can enhance our curriculum from an introductory survey to a rigorous skill-building class by allowing students to practice with hands-on learning.

## IS THERE A RIGHT OR WRONG WAY?

What will be evident throughout this collection is that there are numerous ways to approach the ethics curriculum and build more than just an introductory, advanced, or graduate course. This book provides the roadmap to bolster education across your curriculum. I bring this chapter to a close with an opportunity: The advanced media ethics classroom is a suitable place to provide a space to develop students' resilience.

When we think of educational resilience, we can draw from what Ye et al. (2021)[4] described as "Academic Resilience." The authors define academic resilience as a student's capacity to perform highly despite disadvantages. A disadvantage is the educational environment our students are working through, including the social-emotional and socioeconomic concerns. A disadvantage is also the professional environment our students are working toward in the future. I explore the former later in this book; thus, I intend to address the latter here. Our students will enter professions with ample opportunities to encounter trauma, inequity, and power imbalance issues. Because of this, we need to work toward skills that build resilience. For example, the advanced media ethics course is where we can introduce the concept of trauma and trauma-informed practices and explore the potential places this may occur.

I still remember participating in a ride-along for my reporting class and seeing someone placed in a body bag. I was never trained by my instructor—a newspaper professional—how to encounter something like that, and years later, I can still recreate that image in my head. Beyond my own experience, we can reflect on the images of police brutality: George Floyd, Breonna Taylor, Eric Garner, Tamir Rice, Michael Brown, and Daunte Wright, to name a few. We can think about the erasure of LGBTQIA+ voices, especially those in the transgender community. For many of our students, these are traumatic events and stories that we need to begin to prepare them for, and they must leave our classes with the skills to not only take care of these stories but also themselves.

An introductory-level media ethics course focuses on theoretical concepts and core values of media practice. Still, an advanced-level media ethics course offers the chance for us to bring students into direct conversation with the moment and prepare them to respond to it. This course also gives us a place to encourage student reflection and teach students how to care for themselves. In essence, an advanced-level media ethics course could be designed from an ethic of care and teach students that care is not simply a relationship with others but also a relationship with themselves. Let's build a more resilient media profession and a more sustainable institution that cares about those they serve and themselves.

## NOTES

1. Michael McDowell, "A Framework for Fostering Rigor in PBL: A strategy called hexagonal thinking provides students with an effective way to launch project-based learning," Edutopia, George Lucas Educational Foundation, November 28, 2022, https://www.edutopia.org/article/a-framework-for-fostering-rigor-in-pbl; see also, *Rigorous PBL by Design* (Thousand Oaks, CA: Corwin/SAGE, 2017).

2. "What is Experiential Learning?," Institute for Experiential Learning website, 2021, https://experientiallearninginstitute.org/resources/what-is-experiential-learning/.

3. Aristotle, *Nicomachean Ethics*, translated by Terence Irwin (Indianapolis, IN: Hackett, 1999), 18–19.

4. Wangqiong Ye, Rolf Strietholt, and Sigrid Blömeke, "Academic Resilience: Underlying Norms and Validity of Definitions," *Educational Assessment, Evaluation and Accountability* 33, no. 1 (2021): 169–202, https://link.springer.com/article/10.1007/s11092-020-09351-7.

# 4

# Graduate Seminars in Media Ethics

Ryan J. Thomas, Washington State University

Somebody assigned to teach an undergraduate media ethics class for the first time would not be short of resources to aid them in confronting this task. From reflections and recommendations by senior scholars in the field[1] to a plethora of online resources[2] to empirical studies of best and current practices,[3] such a teacher may well feel less daunted on account of the resources at their fingertips (to which this volume will undoubtedly make a fine addition).

This is emphatically not the case with graduate-level classes in media ethics. Graduate classes have received neither the thoughtful reflection nor the empirical analysis of their undergraduate analogs. This is not a criticism; rather, it reflects inevitability—there are fewer graduate programs to begin with, and across these programs there is enormous variation in scope, curriculum, and objectives.[4] For many programs, a graduate media ethics class may not even be in the course catalog. Yet such classes do exist—I've taught two of them—so we need to think about how one approaches such a task.

This conundrum is one I faced when I was asked to teach the Missouri School of Journalism's graduate-level seminar in media ethics. Readers may be surprised to learn that despite being a pioneer in journalism education and the academic home of some of the most significant scholars in the history of media ethics as a field—Stephanie Craft, Edmund Lambeth, John Merrill, and Lee Wilkins among them—Missouri does *not* have a dedicated undergraduate class in media ethics. But Missouri *does* have a graduate seminar in media ethics, which became part of my teaching rotation a year into my decade as a faculty member there. I went on to teach "J8080" most semesters until I returned to Washington State University (where I received my graduate degrees) in 2022. At WSU, I am now teaching a very different graduate-level course. Examining the differences between these courses is instructive because it highlights a theme I hope to develop in this chapter—the need to know the goals of the students your class serves because this affects every single teaching "move" you make thereafter.

## THE GOALS OF AN ETHICS CLASS

As Daniel Callahan notes, "the very phrase 'the teaching of ethics' has a variety of connotations. . . . One can never be certain just what people hear when they encounter the notion of 'teaching ethics.'"[5] Ethics classes should not be about enumerating "do's and don'ts," as this misses the focus on moral reasoning and the testing of assumptions. Rather, ethics classes should be about stimulating moral imagination, identifying moral issues, developing analytical skills, eliciting a sense of moral obligation, and developing in students a healthy tolerance for disagreement and ambiguity.[6]

Necessarily complicating these goals is the fact that ethics classes outside of philosophy departments tend to have some connection with, or orientation to, a specific profession or vocation, and thus such "applied," "practical," or "professional" ethics courses are designed to address problems common to these fields.[7] In the context of media, the purpose of an ethics class tends to revolve around preparing aspiring journalists, advertisers, public relations professionals, and their like for the ethical challenges that await them in the workplace. Consequently, a "case study" method tends to dominate, where instructors introduce real-world cases faced by professionals and interrogate the conduct of the actors therein.[8] Case studies are certainly useful, but scholars have warned of the dangers of overreliance on them as they can be disconnected from ethics theory[9] and devolve into finger-wagging condemnation of "bad guys" without encouraging much self-reflection on the part of the finger-wagger.[10]

Potential pitfalls notwithstanding, there is much to be said about the nobility of applied ethics education. For media professionals, such classes are essential in posing "why" questions that complement (and occasionally provide an important counterpoint to) the many classes that focus on "how" questions. The assumption in such courses is that media educators are morally obligated to prepare practitioners who are as skilled at moral reasoning as they are at writing, editing, photography, and so on. This, Warren Bovée argues, is essential to the very mission of journalism education, and to lose sight of media practice as something people *do* (and thus must be trained to do *well*) is a betrayal of this mission.[11]

## THE GOALS OF GRADUATE EDUCATION

This becomes complicated at the graduate level, as graduate education has different objectives than undergraduate education. In a 1998 report, the Association of American Universities' Committee on Graduate Education described the purpose of graduate programs in the arts, humanities, and social sciences to "preserve and enlarge our understanding of the history and scope of human thought and the human condition, and transmit that knowledge to succeeding generations," to "inform the public discourse essential to the functioning of a democracy," and to "enhance the capacity of universities to foster national and international intellectual discourse on major . . . debates."[12] It is assumed that a substantial goal of graduate education is preparing future members of the professoriate,[13] and graduate seminars are tailored to expose these emergent academics to specific, substantive areas of literature, such that they can deepen their understanding of these literatures. Consequently, the idea of ethics education as a component of one's professional training for a media career may not *necessarily* apply.

How do we align ethics and graduate education? On the one hand, students "deserve a curriculum tailored for their specific situation."[14] On the other hand, those "specific situations" might vary in the context of graduate-level classes. There is variety across graduate programs in journalism, media, and communication about what graduate education is for, which belies a tacit understanding that whatever permutation it takes, it must be distinct from undergraduate education.[15] The growth of the "alternative-academic" career route notwithstanding,[16] a doctorate has traditionally been seen as a route into the professoriate. Master's students, meanwhile, may or may not be seeking entry into academia, and may be coming to graduate school fresh out of a bachelor's program or with substantial professional (and "life") experience. How does one align these seemingly disparate goals?

## THE CLASSES

To address this question, I turn to my experiences teaching graduate-level ethics at both Missouri and Washington State ("J8080" and "COM 563," respectively). Looking at these very different classes hopefully illuminates some of the challenges and opportunities of graduate media ethics education.

## J8080: Media Ethics

This graduate-level seminar in media ethics is offered most semesters, typically enrolling around 20 students per semester and meeting once a week for two-and-a-half hours. As of this writing, it is one of four classes that all MA students at Missouri must choose from as part of a theoretical "core" around which a largely skills-based curriculum sits (the others being "Communications Law," "Literature of Journalism," and "Philosophy of Journalism"). PhD students can, and do, take it as an elective class. The class pools three distinct student populations: 1) MA students coming straight from a BA program with little to no professional experience; 2) MA students returning to academia after time "in industry," often bringing with them substantial professional chops and seeking either entrance into academia or professional advancement in their field; and 3) PhD students (possessing varying degrees of professional experience) who are, for the most part, seeking a theoretically driven ethics education to deepen their knowledge of media ethics as a field such that they may become a "media ethics scholar" (and, perhaps, media ethics educator).

The first challenge I faced was choosing readings. Because I like the structure that comes with a textbook, I anchored the semester around that textbook's content, with each week of the course focusing on a new chapter from the book. This provided an anchoring topic for that week's discussion (e.g., justice, harm, transparency) that I could build other readings around. I am something of a restless soul, doomed to always make more work for himself than is necessary, so I never fully settled on a single text. Over the course of my time teaching the class I alternated between Patrick Lee Plaisance's *Media Ethics: Key Principles for Responsible Practice*, William W. Neher's *Communicating Ethically: Character, Duties, Consequences, and Relationships*, and Lee Wilkins, Chad Painter, and Philip Patterson's *Media Ethics: Issues and Cases*.[17] All are commendable. I supplemented this with a mix of journal articles (drawing mainly but not exclusively on content published in the *Journal of Media Ethics*) and "case studies" addressing contemporaneous articles highlighting ethics issues (drawing substantially on industry-facing outlets like *Columbia Journalism Review* and *NiemanLab*). The mix between "theory" and "practice" in reading selections ensured that there was something for everyone while also reinforcing a firm rejection of the so-called theory-practice divide.

The class became an important exercise in addressing media ethics' "canonicity problem."[18] In addition to the usual canons of deontology, virtue ethics, and consequentialism, we looked at care ethics, ubuntuism, cultural relativism, and critical theory. I deliberately chose weekly readings that were written by non-US authors or addressed non-US topics (or readings that were both). For students lacking prior coursework in ethics, it was an opportunity to "reset the canon" and present traditions that are often neglected on the same pedestal as the familiar ones. For students with some prior understanding of these theories, it was an opportunity to put these theories in conversation with one another to look at old problems through new lenses.

What helped me pull the different threads of my class together was a common focus on reasoning and argumentation. I set out to encourage students, whatever degree they were seeking, to hone their arguments and challenge their existing assumptions. I wanted students to be comfortable speaking and writing in their own voices and designed assignments to this end. One of these assignments asked students to facilitate a critical discussion of one of the week's journal articles ("critical" defined here as "evaluative," not "negative") which accompanied a short reading notes assignment where students were explicitly forbidden from quoting and had to paraphrase, putting the material into their own words. For their culminating assignment, I asked MA students to write their own code of ethics that integrated their personal and professional values into a set of theoretically coherent "I will" statements to guide their future practice. Students were instructed that the paper must be written in the first person. It helped them see that the value of codes of ethics lies not in the list of directives but in the reasoning that supports them.

Likewise, PhD students were asked to write a final paper that eschewed the typical empirical research study common to graduate courses and instead invited them to argue a particular point in media ethics scholarship. Students reported that this was a difficult assignment; resources abound about empirical research design, but there are far fewer resources in media, journalism, and communication studies about the craft of writing the theoretical essay—with some notable exceptions.[19] In some semesters, I assigned Zachary Seech's very handy "Writing Philosophy Papers" as a supplementary text to aid students in developing these papers,[20] in addition to my own lengthy "style guide" (I confess, I am a very picky editor). Both MA and PhD students routinely reported that they enjoyed the opportunity to stretch themselves, learn a new mode of writing, and write in "their own voice."

What I thought would be a challenge—the distinct populations enrolled—turned out to be one of the class's greatest joys. In addition to having the good fortune of the class attracting significant enrollment from international students (always important in challenging US-centric assumptions) and from students with backgrounds and interests across the media fields (from journalism to strategic communication and beyond), the mix of MA and PhD students turned out to be remarkably generative. Our discussions were by turns grounded and aspirant, with students bringing their perspectives to the mix. The eagerness and zeal of the younger MA students was met with wisdom and humility on the part of industry veterans and PhD students. I wanted to create a space where students could articulate and evaluate their own assumptions, as well as constructively probe the assumptions of others. I felt like students met me in that goal, which made instruction a happy experience.

**COM 563: Ethics for Professionals**

I returned to the Edward R. Murrow College of Communication at Washington State University in 2022 as an associate professor, 10 years after I'd graduated from there with my PhD. One of the classes I was assigned to teach (and am teaching as of this writing) was a class in the college's online MA program for working professionals in strategic and health communication seeking an advanced degree to enable new professional opportunities (whether in their current workplace or beyond). The degree is specifically designated as a professional degree, meaning that students complete a project as their culminating assignment, rather than the traditional academic thesis. This population of students was different from Missouri's insomuch as the students shared key characteristics and goals—they were all MA students, all taking the class online, all seeking professional advancement (rather than academic careers), and all working professionals taking the class in their spare time. The class also raised a different challenge insomuch as I am not a scholar of strategic or health communication (my own research interests focus squarely on journalism).

My starting assumption for this class was that the students were better positioned to connect theory to practice than I was—they were currently working professionals, after all. So, I took as my goal exposing them to theories of ethics that would give them the conceptual toolkit and vocabulary to work through the kinds of issues they may encounter in their respective workplaces and invite them to make these connections in weekly discussion board assignments. I used William W. Neher's *Communicating Ethically: Character, Duties, Consequences, and Relationships*[21] as an anchor, moving through the semester by "touring" four "families" of theories centered around, as the title suggests, character, duties, consequences, and relationships. Around this spine, I built a mix of original source material (e.g., reading Immanuel Kant as part of our module on duties; reading Carol Gilligan as part of our module on relationships) and more contemporaneous academic material. I opted not to choose readings from the popular press, instead asking them to close the theory-practice "gap" themselves by relating the module's readings to their own experiences, workplaces, and ethical dilemmas. Students have risen to the challenge, asking questions about, for example, what it means to be a person of virtuous character in the workplace, the applicability of care in a professional setting, and the familiar tension between ends and means in achieving strategic communications objectives. For their final projects, students are asked to apply what they have learned to a case study they design, present, and discuss. Again, I am seeking students to step forward to make the connection between theory and practice themselves.

## LESSONS LEARNED

What becomes immediately apparent in contrasting the two classes is the need to know the student population you serve. Washington State's COM 563 is what we could call a "dedicated purpose" class, where the students enrolled are all broadly seeking the same goal. Missouri's J8080, on the other hand, is more of a "multiple purpose" class, where the students enrolled may have different career objectives. I believe that graduate teaching in ethics must meet students where they are in terms of the goals they are seeking for their degree and tailor their instruction accordingly. Doing so harmonizes the course content and the student experience.

There is, however, a "common core" to ethics classes that I believe holds true whether the student population has lots of professional experience or none, whether they intend on becoming a journalist or a journalism scholar. Indeed, this core also connects graduate classes to undergraduate classes. The core lies in the ability to articulate one's values while being open to their modification, identify the moral contours of a given issue while discerning the weight of competing options, recognize the factors that enable and constrain ethical decision-making, and become mindful listeners who recognize the productive tension of disagreement. Those are goals to which I believe every ethics class should aspire.

## NOTES

1. See, for example, Sandra L. Borden, "Avoiding the Pitfalls of Case Studies," *Journal of Mass Media Ethics* 13, no. 1 (1998): 5–13, https://doi.org/10.1207/s15327728jmme1301_1; Clifford G. Christians, "Media Ethics in Education," *Journalism and Communication Monographs* 9, no. 4 (2007): 179–221, https://doi.org/10.1177/152263790800900402; Wendy N. Wyatt, "The Humble yet Lofty Goals of a Journalism Ethics Course," in *The Routledge Companion to Journalism Ethics*, edited by Lada Trifonova Price, Karen Sanders, and Wendy N. Wyatt (New York: Routledge, 2021), 504–12.

2. See, for example, the case studies, syllabi, and class activities provided by the University of Wisconsin–Madison's Center for Journalism Ethics.

3. See, for example, Jacob Groshek and Michael Conway, "The Effectiveness of the Pervasive Method in Ethics Pedagogy: A Longitudinal Study of

Journalism and Mass Communication Students," *Journalism* 14, no. 3 (2013): 330–47, https://doi.org/10.1177/1464884912454503; Edmund B. Lambeth, Clifford Christians, and Kyle Cole, "Role of the Media Ethics Course in the Education of Journalists," *Journalism Educator* 49, no. 3 (1994): 20–26, https://doi.org/10.1177/107769589404900303; Edmund B. Lambeth, Clifford G. Christians, Kenneth Fleming, and Seow Ting Lee, "Media Ethics Teaching in Century 21: Progress, Problems, and Challenges," *Journalism and Mass Communication Educator* 59, no. 3 (2004): 239–358, https://doi.org/10.1177/107769580405900304.

4. Wolfgang Donsbach and Tom Fiedler, "Journalism School Curriculum Enrichment: A Midterm Report of the Carnegie-Knight Initiative on the Future of Journalism Education" (Cambridge, MA: Shorenstein Center on Media, Politics, and Public Policy, Harvard University, 2008), http://shorensteincenter.org/wp-content/uploads/2012/03/journalism_school_curriculum_enrichment_2008.pdf.

5. Daniel Callahan, "Goals in the Teaching of Ethics," in *Ethics Teaching in Higher Education*, edited by Daniel Callahan and Sissela Bok (New York: Plenum, 1980), 61–80.

6. Callahan, "Goals in the Teaching of Ethics"; Christians, "Media Ethics in Education"; Clifford G. Christians and Catherine L. Covert, *Teaching Ethics in Journalism Education* (Hastings-on-Hudson, NY: Hastings Center, 1980).

7. Michael Davis, *Ethics and the University* (New York: Routledge, 1999).

8. Groshek and Conway, "The Effectiveness of the Pervasive Method in Ethics Pedagogy"; Lambeth, Christians, and Cole, "Role of the Media Ethics Course in the Education of Journalists."

9. Borden, "Avoiding the Pitfalls of Case Studies."

10. Deni Elliott, *Ethics in the First Person: A Guide to Teaching and Learning Practical Ethics* (Lanham, MD: Rowman & Littlefield, 2007).

11. Warren G. Bovée, *Discovering Journalism* (Westport, CT: Greenwood, 1999).

12. "AAU Committee on Graduate Education Report and Recommendations" (Washington, DC: Association of American Universities, 1998), https://www.aau.edu/key-issues/aau-committee-graduate-education-report-and-recommendations, 8–9.

13. Carol J. Pardun, Robert McKeever, Geah N. Pressgrove, and Brooke Weberling McKeever, "Colleagues in Training: How Senior Faculty View Doctoral Education," *Journalism and Mass Communication Educator* 70, no. 4 (2015): 354–66, https://doi.org/10.1177/1077695815599471.

14. Ronald R. Sims, *Teaching Business Ethics for Effective Learning* (Westport, CT: Quorum, 2002), 28.

15. Donsbach and Fiedler, "Journalism School Curriculum Enrichment."

16. Kevin Kelly, Kathryn E. Linder, and Thomas J. Tobin, *Going Alt-Ac: A Guide to Alternative Academic Careers* (Sterling, VA: Stylus, 2020).

17. William W. Neher, *Communicating Ethically: Character, Duties, Consequences, and Relationships*, 3rd edition (New York: Routledge, 2020); Patrick Lee Plaisance, *Media Ethics: Key Principles for Responsible Practice*, 2nd edition (Thousand Oaks, CA: SAGE, 2014); Lee Wilkins, Chad Painter, and Philip Patterson, *Media Ethics: Issues and Cases*, 10th edition (Lanham, MD: Rowman & Littlefield, 2021).

18. Christians, "Media Ethics in Education," 186.

19. See, for example, Judee K. Burgoon, "The Challenge of Writing the Theoretical Essay," in *How to Publish Your Communication Research: An Insider's Guide*, edited by Alison Alexander and W. James Potter (Thousand Oaks, CA: SAGE, 2001), 47–56; Stephen D. Reese, "Writing the Conceptual Article: A Practical Guide," *Digital Journalism* 11, no. 7 (2023): 1195-210, https://doi.org/10.1080/21670811.2021.2009353.

20. Zachary Seech, *Writing Philosophy Papers*, 5th edition (Belmont, CA: Wadsworth, 2009).

21. Neher, *Communicating Ethically.*

# 5

# Diversifying the Ethics Curriculum

Chad Painter, University of Dayton

Diversity matters in media ethics education, because it matters in the broader field of mass communication. Learning about diversity enables students to understand issues across cultures, which is vital in an interconnected, global political and economic world. Diversity education also helps students navigate US societal shifts, such as the transition from Baby Boomers to Generations X, Y, and Z; changing fertility and immigration trends; and fluctuating living patterns and values. Students also can better understand cultural history in terms of race and ethnicity; biological sex, gender, and sexual orientation; and socioeconomic class—among many other aspects.

Media ethics and other mass communication courses can—and often do—address diversity in multiple ways.[1] Examples of how diversity can be included in classes include assignments, clients, guest speakers, and content—including content created by people with nondominant identities, as well as content about people of nondominant identities.

## INCORPORATING DIVERSITY IN MEDIA ETHICS COURSES

Diversity-oriented learning outcomes or aims can be included in syllabi.[2] For example, my syllabus for an undergraduate, standalone media ethics course includes the following learning-outcome language: "Students will be able to explain their own views and ethical reasoning in terms that diverse groups of people can understand." Even stronger language, though, could be included. Example language could include learning outcomes such as "to learn skills to be an effective journalism professional in a global community" and "to challenge assumptions about cultural groups and to learn how to reach diverse audiences."

Journalists, broadcasters, and strategic communicators will encounter social problems (e.g., racism, homophobia, anti-Semitism, Islamophobia) during their careers, so it is vital for journalism and mass communication programs to find ways for students to talk about, think about, and wrestle with issues surrounding diversity and diverse audiences.[3] This talking, thinking, and wrestling with challenging ideas and cases often is the heart of a media ethics course. The role of media ethics is vital to remember as universities increasingly inject more digital skills courses (e.g., social media engagement, analytics, data visualization), necessitating the deemphasis or jettisoning of more traditional courses such as media ethics.[4] One survey found that 91 percent of US-based, accredited journalism and mass communication programs offered a freestanding ethics course, though only 71 percent required students to take it. Further, only 10 out of 119 programs offered a course with both "ethics" and "diversity" in the title, and just five programs required it.[5]

## INCLUSION OF THE FAULT LINES APPROACH

Faculty could adopt the Maynard Institute's "fault lines" approach that emphasizes intersectionality.[6] Robert Maynard originally conceived of five fault lines: race and ethnicity, class, gender and sexual orientation, geography, and generation. Subsequent scholars have expanded the list to include religion, disability, and political affiliation as potential fault lines.[7] Maynard argued that we, as journalists and members of society, cannot and should not pretend that differences do not exist. The key, then, is providing context and history. That context and history occurs through understanding and using fault lines. For journalists, fault lines can better help them reflect the interests, decisions, and actions of sources in a different social group. Fault lines also can provide a way to identify missing cultural voices, as well as story angles and perspectives that could offer a way to reframe a story or add complexity. The questions to ask: What fault lines are reflected in my sources, and how do those fault lines affect their comments, interests, decisions, or actions? Arguably more importantly, what fault lines are missing, and are they needed to help readers better understand the relevance of the information?

The "fault lines" approach can be integrated seamlessly into course content. My "Potter Box" lecture begins with an in-depth discussion of the four components of the ethical decision-making tool: 1) the empirical definition, or understanding the morally relevant facts of the case, 2) outlining values, 3) application of the philosophical principles, and 4) articulation of loyalties. The class then shifts to an application of the Potter Box using an example of a September 2, 2015, photograph published in the British newspaper *The Independent* showing the body of a Syrian refugee found after the child drowned during the journey from Turkey to Greece. The picture graphically shows the refugee, Alan Kurdi, a 2-year-old Syrian boy who drowned along with his mother and brother while attempting to flee the Syrian Civil War. To discuss the Potter Box, I begin students with this prompt:

> You are magically transported to September 1, 2015. You are the chief editor of the *Detroit Free Press*, the daily newspaper in a major American city with a large Syrian population. The dilemma you face is whether to publish the same photo in your paper. Use the Potter Box to address the journalistic ethical issues related to this photo, and make a decision about what your paper will publish (if anything) regarding the photo, its placement, the headline, and the story.

For students to fully wrestle with the ethical dilemma, they have to address several fault lines, including race and ethnicity (e.g., students can compare and contrast similar decisions, such as the 2019 photo of Óscar Alberto Martínez Ramírez and his daughter Valeria, Salvadoran migrants who drowned in the Rio Grande), generation (e.g., would the decision be different if the photo was of an adult rather than a child?), and geography (e.g., would the decision be different if the boy in the photo was American, or how does the large Syrian population in Detroit influence your decision of whether or not to show the photo?).

## INCLUDING DIVERSITY IN ASSIGNMENTS

Faculty could require inclusion of diverse populations in assignments.[8] Position papers are one commonly used assignment, and they could serve as a good way to introduce diversity into the course. In my classes, I include three position papers spread throughout the semester. In my position paper assignment, the students' ethical rationale for their position must include at least two ethical traditions or philosophers. They also cannot reuse a philosopher in subsequent papers. So, for example, if the student wrote about Immanuel Kant in the first paper and wanted to focus on truth-telling again, that student could instead focus on Sissela Bok. The same idea could hold for virtue ethics (e.g., Aristotle or Confucius), privacy (e.g., Margaret Jane Radin's concept of contested communities or *hezzek re'iyyah* in Talmudic law), social justice (e.g., Amartya Sen's social choice theory or Martha Nussbaum's capabilities approach), and moral development (e.g., Carol Gilligan), as well as more applied philosophy (e.g., Sherry Baker's TARES test for strategic communication and Patricia Werhane's work on stakeholder theory for media economics).

Faculty also can introduce diversity into the position prompts. My first position paper is almost always adapted from Brian Simmons' "Hate Radio: The Outer Limits of Tasteful Broadcasting," which focuses on a fictional radio talk-show host who is criticized—probably correctly—for being "offensive, tasteless, rude, racist, obscene, and insensitive." The task for students is to decide whether to keep the popular-but-controversial radio host on the air. (We also talk through Aristotle's "middle path" and discuss a range of alternatives between the two extremes of either firing the radio host or leaving him on the air without any repercussions.) As previously stated, students will encounter social problems once they enter the field, so it's important for students to begin the process of thinking through these issues in the relatively safe space of a media ethics classroom.[9] Other position papers have students focus on editorial decisions in the film *Spotlight* (which often is especially poignant to my students, who are at a Catholic university); and the *New York Post*'s 2012 "Doomed" front cover, which delves into race and ethnicity (the victim, alleged perpetrator, and photographer are all non-white) and mental illness. This list is far from exhaustive; the University of Texas Center for Media Engagement and the University of Wisconsin–Madison's Center for Journalism Ethics both have good lists of case studies that easily could be turned into position paper assignments.

## PARTNERING WITH ORGANIZATIONS

Faculty could develop partnerships with organizations that serve non-dominant and marginalized groups.[10] Most cities and communities have a wide variety of advocacy organizations; members of these groups could be good guest lecturers, and these groups could offer service-learning opportunities for students. Further, these types of organizations typically are pretty easy to find. For example, Dayton Serves (an aggregating site for organizations in Dayton, where I live) features groups centered on social justice and equality, hunger, poverty, senior services, and veterans—just to name a few.

A related concept is to develop partnerships with news and strategic communication organizations. Cristina Bodinger-de Uriarte and Gunnar Valgeirsson,[11] in an interview study of 613 US journalists, found that those journalists generally perceived news organizations as giving low priority to staff diversity, saw minority advancement as problematic, did not view diversity as an ethical imperative, and did not believe diversity represented an important aspect of their own work or personal responsibility. There is a possibility for collaboration between media ethics classrooms and newspaper newsrooms, for example, on the topic of historical racial coverage. Several newspapers—including the *Kansas City Star, Baltimore Sun, Los Angeles Times, Philadelphia Inquirer,* and *Golden Transcript (Colorado)*—have issued apologies to readers following historical analyses of race coverage in their papers. Similarly, students could do a deep dive into their campus media coverage of diversity following the textual analysis and focus group model developed by Teri Finneman, Marina Hendricks, and Piotr Bobkowski.[12]

## SERVICE LEARNING

Faculty could create a service-learning project opportunity in an underserved community.[13] I like to have students read Robert Coles' essay "The Disparity Between Intellect and Character." Coles argues that "Institutions originally founded to teach their students how to become good and decent, as well as broadly and deeply literate, may abandon the first mission to concentrate on a driven, narrow book learning."[14] In other words, there is a disconnect between moral reasoning (knowing good) and moral conduct (trying to become a good person). One way to bridge that gap is through a service-learning project. Service learning can take many forms from direct service (e.g., students volunteering at a local food bank), to indirect service (e.g., fundraising for a cause), advocacy (e.g., speaking out for a cause), and research (e.g., collecting data or conducting surveys to better understand an issue). Service learning does not have to be massive and time-consuming. My students discuss St. Thérèse of Lisieux's concept of the "little way." Ordinary acts—as simple as a sincere and gracious thank you to the people serving food in the student union—could be an act of doing good.

As another example, many students rarely encounter poverty firsthand, and, even in news writing, often limit contact with poor people due to developing their skills by telling stories on campus.[15] The same is true for many other communities that do not share demographics with the dominant culture. One way to counteract the sequestering that often happens on a college campus is to incorporate the "listening post" assignment, which is common in basic news writing courses but easily could be adapted for the media ethics curriculum. In a "listening post," students are encouraged to find communities that are uncovered, under-covered, under-served, and under-researched (e.g., elder care facility, a cultural center that focuses on an under-reported group, an ethnic store, a church of a religion to which the student doesn't belong, a veterans' center, a social service facility, after-school programs) and "listen" with all five senses by having conversations, taking in the sights and smells, reading bulletin boards, etc. I tell students the purpose of the exercise is to "encourage you to stretch beyond your comfort zone to experience a cultural group that you are not familiar with and that typically goes underreported or is not understood well. The instructions for the assignment are intended to help you choose 'listening posts' that will facilitate those types of uncomfortable and/or unfamiliar cross-cultural experiences." Motley and Sturgill[16] found that exposure to diversity could potentially help create professionals who are more respectful and sensitive to marginalized populations.

## DIVERSITY THROUGHOUT THE CURRICULUM

A professor—in coordination with other departments, colleges, and/or university faculty—could incorporate diversity issues throughout the curriculum with at least one module or major assignment. One important aspect of diversity education is that the most effective teaching of diversity content must be integrated throughout the curriculum—not just in one course or across a few electives.[17] The best practice is to infuse diversity into a variety of courses, including theory, skills, survey and foundational, ethics and law, research, and critical-thinking oriented classes.[18]

A second component is experiential learning through campus media organizations (e.g., newspapers, TV and radio stations, public relations firms). Diversity training ideally would begin as an ethical imperative; classroom education and campus media could partner to develop practical expectations and strategies for diverse coverage that would later transfer to the industry when students become working journalists. However, student media often face the same diversity criticisms as their professional counterparts—often but not exclusively due to insufficient minority representation in student media—indicating that higher education also is falling short.[19]

## CONCLUDING THOUGHTS

This chapter began with the argument that diversity education matters throughout the realm of mass communication. Media ethics is a logical place to include diversity discussions, and many of the leading textbooks (e.g., Christians, Fackler, Brittain, Richardson, and Kreshel's *Media Ethics: Cases and Moral Reasoning*; Wilkins, Painter, and Patterson's *Media Ethics: Issues and Cases*; Plaisance's *Media Ethics: Key Principles for Responsible*

*Practice*; and the Society of Professional Journalists' *Media Ethics: A Guide for Professional Conduct*) include dedicated chapters or large sections on social justice and diversity issues.

There are a multitude of ways to include diversity in a media ethics classroom. I included five here: learning outcomes, inclusion of the fault lines approach, including diversity in assignments, partnering with organizations, and service learning. Additionally, diversity should not be solely siloed into media ethics; instead, diversity should be incorporated throughout the curriculum.

Throughout, I've included examples of classroom-tested content and assignments. Including all might seem overwhelming—and rightly so. Adding one or two a semester can improve a media ethics course, especially in terms of diversity content. Further, the included content and assignments are not meant to be exhaustive; indeed, there is a wealth of good work being done in media ethics classrooms throughout the United States and globally. Many of those can be found at https://ethics.journalism.wisc.edu/resources/resources-for-teachers-students/. Your good ideas can and should be included on that site.

## NOTES

1. Masudul Biswas, Elliot King, April Newton, and Nguyên Nguyên, "Addressing Diversity Across the Communication Curriculum: A Case Study," *Teaching Journalism and Mass Communication* 12, no. 1 (2022): 26; Margaretha Geertsema-Sligh, Ingrid Bachmann, and Mia Moody-Ramirez, "Educating Journalism Students on Gender and Inequality," *Journalism and Mass Communication Educator* 75, no. 1 (2020): 72–73; Phillip Motley and Amanda Sturgill, "Cultivating a Professional Ethic in Covering Marginalized Populations: Learning About the Poor through Service-Learning," *Journalism and Mass Communication Educator* 69, no. 2 (2014): 175.

2. Biswas et al., "Addressing Diversity," 26.

3. Biswas et al., "Addressing Diversity," 27.

4. Andrew Mills, Amy Kristin Sanders, and Shakir Shahid Hussain, "Fitting It All In? A Census of Undergraduate Ethics and Leadership Courses in Accredited U.S. Journalism and Mass Communication Programs," *Journalism and Mass Communication Educator* 74, no. 3 (2018): 266.

5. Mills, Sanders, and Hussain, "Fitting It All In," 271.

6. Biswas et al., "Addressing Diversity," 26.

7. See "Robert C. Maynard: Life and Legacy," Maynard Institute, accessed April 21, 2023, http://mije.org.

8. Biswas et al., "Addressing Diversity," 26.

9. Biswas et al., "Addressing Diversity," 26.

10. Biswas et al., "Addressing Diversity," 26.

11. Cristina Bodinger-de Uriarte and Gunnar Valgeirsson, "Institutional Disconnects as Obstacles to Diversity in Journalism in the United States," *Journalism Practice* 9, no. 3 (2015): 411–13.

12. Teri Finneman, Marina Hendricks, and Piotr Bobkowski, "'The Paper is White': Examining Diversity Issues with the Next Generation of Journalists," *Journalism and Mass Communication Educator* 77, no. 2 (2022): 222.

13. Biswas et al., "Addressing Diversity," 26.

14. Robert Coles, "The Disparity Between Intellect and Character," *Chronicle of Higher Education*, September 22, 1995, https://www.chronicle.com/article/the-disparity-between-intellect-and-character/.

15. Motley and Sturgill, "Cultivating a Professional Ethic," 167.

16. Motley and Sturgill, "Cultivating a Professional Ethic," 166–79.

17. Masudul Biswas and Ralph Izard, "Infusing Diversity Content Across the Curriculum," *Teaching Journalism and Mass Communication* 8, no. 1 (2018): 2.

18. Biswas and Izard, "Infusing Diversity," 1.

19. Finneman, Hendricks, and Bobkowski, "The Paper is White," 223.

# 6

# Inclusive Teaching as Ethical Practice

Patrick R. Johnson, Marquette University

Most teacher preparation for postsecondary education focuses on traditional curricular and instructional concerns. This book represents pedagogical decisions journalism and mass communication educators can make regarding ethics education. When preparing new instructors, we often overlook a consideration of self and the role of inclusion in our choices. This chapter brings forth that idea by helping journalism and mass communication educators think about how inclusive practices are an ethical imperative in our teaching. I explore two different opportunities in this chapter: inclusive consideration and self-reflection. Inclusive consideration explores ways to make our classroom spaces accessible and a place where students feel they belong. Self-reflection implies a positionality and an awareness of how one's privilege or marginalization influences curriculum design, instructional strategies, and student reception. I begin in the same place as our classes: opening day.

## WHO DO YOU WANT TO BE?

The first day of class usually includes introductions and the syllabus. In those introductions, we typically ask some variation of "Why are you here?" While the question doesn't inherently imply harm, what it does do is require students to defend their place—and sometimes their worth—in the class. Responses then include a variation of "because the topic sounded fun" or "because it's required to be here." And where does that get us? What do we learn about the budding media professionals in our classes? The beginning of our journey to a more inclusive pedagogy is to shift the question from the start.

By shifting the question, we ask students to share their futures and what they imagine them to look like. Instead of focusing on one's place in class, the focus becomes on their place in the world around them. This also reveals something about you. Students see that what you value isn't just the course content but the role students are willing to play in how that content is used in the present and their futures. You can then learn something richer about your students, which can be used to structure more inclusive practices. Implementing a different questioning style on the first day of class can also impact how we present the syllabus to our students.

The syllabus represents a "living contract" with our students. We often joke that "it's in the syllabus," because we consistently find ourselves using that response when students ask questions. Yet we don't often ask the question why? Why don't students engage (I'm avoiding using read here on purpose) with the syllabus? My students want more interactivity between their technologies and the syllabus, such as setting calendar notifications, adding hyperlinks, and sharing additional readings and resources. I like to include resources within the learning management systems (LMS) version of my syllabus that help address remediation, an essential consideration for inclusion. Beyond the "students don't read the syllabus" conversation or the "it doesn't reflect how I learn" response, we need to push ourselves to rethink the syllabus from a lens of inclusivity. For example, what kind of inclusivity statement is presented? Is it the one supplied by your university or department? In my conversations with students, they often share that they *know* when a syllabus is nothing more than boilerplate language. In a recent course, students shared that only seeing DEI statements from departments or the university made them feel like it wasn't valued; it was simply information all faculty must include. Even in political contention in education, it is essential to share your classroom positionality and how you intend to approach inclusive learning in your classes through the language of your syllabus. And then it should be clear in your curricular decision-making that you uphold that.

## HOW CAN MY CLASSROOM BE A PLACE FOR ALL?

Beyond asking students who they want to be, we should consider how we design our classes to ensure the inclusion of all students. When we create classes, the ethical imperatives of diversity, equity, and inclusion should be central to our mission. But how? And, in some circles, there may be questions of why. DEI means recognizing that our classroom spaces are a place for being seen, feeling heard, and knowing we all belong. Inclusion can be accomplished in several ways, but I've highlighted three that may be useful to any classroom. I've also used several examples that instructors can implement in an ethics class immediately after reading this chapter. These strategies include incorporating diverse voices, providing alternate or multiple assessment forms, and creating accessible materials and inclusive activities.

### Diverse Voices

One of the easiest ways to be inclusive is to incorporate diverse voices into your curriculum. This means ensuring that you include a variety of races, ethnicities, genders, sexualities, ages, and geographies. For example, if you teach an introductory ethics course, you have non-Western philosophies like Daoism or Confucianism. Or you make sure that feminist standpoint theory or care ethics are included in the class. It also means being conscious of including diverse identities in the curriculum and avoiding tokenizing the voices.

Starting by adding more content into a course to enhance diversity and representation can muddy the curriculum. Addition without subtraction can lead to overcrowding. The overcrowding then doesn't allow students to engage critically with diverse voices. Instead, it can become a representation for representation's sake. Adding diverse voices also does not mean highlighting them in a singular week. For example, isolating Black/brown voices or female voices to one week and labeling them as "diversity" weeks (or a variation that focuses on the identity labels) doesn't promote inclusivity. Again, that can become a representation for representation's sake. Increasing your diversity in voices means thinking about international authors, especially those from the Global South. Students often don't encounter these voices independently if we don't share them.

Being more inclusive in your class requires more steps than adding voices. Beyond the texts, think about whose voices are absent and help students to uncover them—including their own. But assume that their previous exposure isn't enough. The journey to discover inclusivity has its barriers, so we must create inclusive instructional practices to help students access our curriculum.

### Alternate Assessments and Multiple Intelligences

Representations aren't the only way to build inclusivity into our teaching. We translate our educational experiences into our teaching practices, which also means our assessment practices and experiences. The most common major assessments in classes are exams and papers. Yet both are somewhat limiting when we consider how students learn. Embedding inclusivity means thinking about how students comprehend your content and how they can perform it proficiently. Take Howard Gardner's multiple intelligences framework.[1] In it, he explains that learners approach tasks in a variety of ways and that these ways don't necessarily have clear-cut criteria for when someone may use one over another. Gardner believes it is essential to design learning experiences that allow different learning styles to show how they approached and comprehended the task. These styles/intelligences include:

- Verbal-linguistic
- Logical-mathematical
- Visual-spatial
- Musical
- Naturalistic
- Bodily-kinesthetic
- Interpersonal
- Intrapersonal

With each style, students process learning differently. If we think about how we design our assessments in our classes, we should consider that there can be multiple ways for students to showcase their knowledge. In ethics classes, we tend to favor verbal-linguistic, interpersonal, and intrapersonal learning. But we need to recognize that only some of our students can engage in those forms. We can include more students in the learning by offering different assessments to achieve the same instructional objectives.

If you traditionally assign a research paper for the final assessment in your class, think about what goals you are trying to achieve. You could have a rubric that helps students to see what those goals are or what outcomes they are being measured by or assessed with. Is the research paper the only way to use that rubric? One way to become more inclusive is to vary your assessment opportunities. Yes, this means additional labor up front, but the outcome is more rewarding for you and your students. Let's still assign that research paper, but instead of just the paper, let's give students options to write a journalistic story, create a podcast episode(s), design a magazine spread, shoot a photo narrative, or outline a campaign. By offering students more options and aligning them to the same evaluation tool (i.e., a rubric), students can pick how they want to perform. In doing so, they can also use the intelligences they've learned as strengths to showcase their proficiency on class objectives.

## Accessible Materials and Activities

When we think about how to be more inclusive in our teaching, there is often a hierarchy in our minds of what to address and how. Unfortunately, that means we may neglect the need to consider accessibility. Many of our students will come to our classrooms with different learning styles (as noted previously), and with those will come different needs. In some cases, students will have barriers to learning that they are working to overcome, while others must seek additional support to navigate how they learn. Students are also entering classrooms with lower testing scores or writing abilities. Keep in mind that not all students will disclose having learning difficulties or ask for accommodations, which makes it imperative to think about possibilities for all students. And many of the accessibility shifts you make can be done in service of all students in your classroom.

Integrating multimodal teaching is one of the most common changes we can make in our classrooms. This includes providing voice-overs for slide decks, using assistive technologies to increase functionality, adding alternative text to visuals, and using closed captioning when delivering audio content. Universal Design for Learning (UDL) is a way to think through early accommodation changes in your curriculum. UDL provides a framework to give all students learning opportunities by thinking about engagement, representation, and expression—the why, what, and how of our learning. Each layer of UDL focuses on options to stimulate motivation, sustain enthusiasm, present information differently, and offer support so learning can happen for all. UDL guidelines recommend seven principles in their Universal Instructional Design Implementation Guide:[2]

- Be accessible and fair.
- Provide flexibility in use, participation, and presentation.
- Be straightforward and consistent.
- Be explicitly presented and readily perceived.
- Provide a supportive learning environment.
- Minimize unnecessary physical effort or requirements.
- Ensure learning spaces that accommodate both students and instructional methods.

Another accessibility opportunity is consistency. We can include accessibility resources on our syllabi and reiterate how we reinforce them, establish common lesson structures and reminders, and encourage reflection and communication about learning experiences. LMSs are suitable places to have a space where all this occurs. For example, while your syllabus in print form doesn't reflect the philosophy of "syllabus as a living document," the LMS can become the living contract with more frequent updates. Students often have phone and SMS notifications from the LMS set, making it a more direct place to share up-to-date information. I create modules for each class session on my LMS. From there, I build a three-part lesson structure to help students see how the class will progress:

- Prepare: Share with students what they will do to prepare for class and what you will do in the course's opening minutes to set the lesson's tone.
- Engage: Share what students will do in class, including the overarching activity and any goals you hope to accomplish.
- Reflect: Share with students how you will transition from the lesson to what they must do to 1) conclude class and 2) transform their learning through an assessment or the upcoming reading assignment.

This structure comes from the learning framework of Project CRISS (CReating Independence through Student-owned Strategies). The design helps students see how learning will develop and how to recognize what types of learning they will be doing at different times. Providing structure for all students encourages equity while reflecting a desire for a more inclusive and common language. Beyond that, remember that an LMS needs to be accessible to all learners; therefore, visit the National Center on Disability and Access to Education website[3] to learn the most effective ways to make your LMS accessible for visual and verbal needs. Suppose you feel uncertain about how best to make your classroom more accessible. In that case, university offices of teaching and learning and disabilities services will have professional development and mentoring opportunities to coach you to be more comfortable.

Another consideration for media teachers is technology or material access. Access for inclusivity doesn't just focus on a learner; it also reflects a need to remember what materials and technologies our students have easy access to when we design assignments and activities. For example, if you have a photo editing assignment, is lab access available for students who don't have editing capabilities on their computers? Or, for an interview assignment, if you require students to do an in-person interview, do students have the resources to get there? Given the importance of technology in our programs, accessibility of resources should be a top priority not just in our classes but also for leadership.

## WHO DO I WANT TO BE?

Once we've thought about what we can do to make our curriculum and instruction more inclusive, we need to take one more step: self-reflection.

This chapter began by sharing one specific instance of a class that we can change to make the remainder of the course feel more inclusive. I then explained how we could use different strategies throughout our class to develop more inclusive pedagogy. But once we're done designing or teaching a class, we often forget to reflect on our experience.

Just as I started by sharing that we should ask students who they want to be, it is essential to conclude with the same question, asking it of ourselves. Who do we want to be? And when we think about that, consider the impact we want on our current and future students. Do we want to be remembered simply for the content, or are we hoping to walk away from an activity, a unit, or a class wanting students to recognize the lasting lessons? If we want the latter, we must reflect on the inclusivity of our courses. Use these questions to reflect on the lesson you taught, the unit you designed, or the course you just completed:

- Who are the voices in my class—both in the curriculum and physically in the classroom?
- Where are these voices located?
- Am I providing students with options that reflect their learning strengths?
- How am I assessing student learning?
- What words am I using in my feedback?
- What kind of access do my students need to be successful in this course?
- What materials or technologies am I using, and how are students expected to use them?
- Do I provide a space for feedback?
- How are students expected to interact with their classmates?
- What types of activities am I using to encourage inclusion and belonging?

Beyond those questions, it is essential to ask ourselves questions. Try these:

- Where do I stand in the room—physically, academically, emotionally, and mentally?
- What do I believe about teaching and learning? And what do I value?
- How do I approach teaching?
- How do students come to know me?
- Who do I want to be?

Integrating self-reflection can be done in several places in your class. I reflect after each lesson. However, for some, it occurs at the end of the class when reflecting on our course experience seems more natural. Regardless of choice, you should consistently integrate self-reflection, such as quarterly or at the midterm.

## INCLUSIVITY AS A CORE PROMISE

This book offers ways to integrate ethics into existing courses or teach standalone ethics classes in your department, school, or college. How you take up the advice in this book is personal, much like teaching. That means what we choose to do in our classes represents a series of essential and interlinked decisions informed by who we are as people and who we want our students to be when they leave our classes.

This chapter provides different approaches to making the experience of being in your class more inclusive, thus amplifying the ethical imperative to support diversity, equity, and inclusion. This chapter represents a sense of belonging that instructors can craft through different pedagogical decisions. It begins with how you frame the course—the question you ask students to justify their belonging in the classroom. From there, it becomes a question of how students experience this course and where they feel they are seen and heard. But none of this is possible without considering how our schools and classrooms will become more diverse as time progresses. Our classrooms will continue to be rich patchwork quilts. Therefore, it will be increasingly essential to undergird our curriculum with inclusivity. So, who do you want to be? And how does that person help create imagined, equitable, and just futures for our students—present and future?

## NOTES

1. "A Beginners Guide to MI," MI Oasis, Harvard Graduate School of Education, accessed April 17, 2023, https://www.multipleintelligencesoasis.org/a-beginners-guide-to-mi.

2. Jaellayna Palmer and Aldo Caputo, *The Universal Instructional Design Implementation Guide* (University of Guelph: Teaching Support Services, 2003), https://ctei.jhu.edu/files/uid-implementation-guide-v6.pdf.

3. "Cheatsheets," National Center on Disability and Access to Education website, 2023, https://ncdae.org/resources/cheatsheets/.

# II

# ETHICS IN EVERY AREA OF STUDY

# 7

# Developing a Combined Media Law and Ethics Course

Jack Breslin, Iona University

A class of undergraduate mass communication majors slowly wanders into their seats for the first class of the semester, and students silently bury their faces in their cell phones. Some students may be looking forward to the experience after enjoying a previous course with you. The majority, however, may be dreading taking this required combined course of media law and media ethics. They have heard that this is a difficult course with lots of required reading and written assignments.

Some of their peers in other schools take media law and media ethics separately—15 weeks (or less) for each. But your school combines the two subjects in 15 (or less) intense weeks.[1] You face the challenge of convincing students about the value of media law and media ethics for their lives and careers. You also must squeeze what your colleagues at other programs teach in two separate courses into one combined course. Some of you might have to convince your department colleagues that your course should be required, not an elective. For decades, my combined course was mandatory for all our majors, but this year my department demoted it to elective status.

What happens when professors combine those two usually standalone courses into one? An exact 50–50 percent split between the two can be difficult, so one of the disciplines may suffer—likely ethics. A panel of combined course professors at the 2022 Association for Education in Journalism and Mass Communication Annual Conference in Detroit, who were mostly law focused, agreed that ethics usually gets the short end.[2]

Where do you make the split—seven weeks of law, seven weeks of ethics, then a concluding hybrid week of common ground? Or after an introductory week of law and another week of ethics, do you cover the legal and ethical aspects of selected topics (e.g., truth-telling, privacy, offensive speech, etc.)? Do you focus on legal-ethical concerns for mass media professions (e.g., journalism, public relations, advertising, digital and visual media, etc.) after the introductions?

The professor's academic or professional background can guide what gets more attention. Some are stronger in law; some are more versed in ethics. A select group specializes in both. For example, when a former chair decided to add a third section to our combined course, she hired a local telecom company attorney with no ethics background. After politely listening over lunch to my suggestions for teaching ethics, he reportedly told his class, "Those who know something about teaching this course say that you can't teach both law and ethics together, so we'll just do law." Even after the chair reminded him of my ethics suggestions, he still focused on one Supreme Court decision after another.

Unless students have plans for law school or enjoy legal studies, they might have concerns about having to study media law. These future mass media practitioners argue that they will work for companies with an army of lawyers to protect them from litigation. Or if they own their own company or work freelance, they will hire some legal eagle to advise them. But that doesn't always happen. One former student, a rising TV reporter at a top-five station in the nation's No. 1 market, learned the hard way. After a careless edit resulted in a settled libel suit that nearly ended his career, he told me, "Maybe I should have paid better attention in your class and kept my notes."

Those students who have not taken a course in philosophy or applied ethics might be misinformed about a mass media ethics course. Aren't media and ethics a contradiction in terms since the American media have no ethics? Some students conclude that media ethics focuses on forming an ethical identity and making ethical decisions in mass media based on one's moral foundation, so how can the professor mark your answer wrong? Your ethical answer is your opinion, which is neither right nor wrong, unless based on fabricated facts. They will soon discover that ethical decisions involve more than emotion, opinion, common sense, or logic, even though those elements can play a role. The name of the course is media law and ethics, not media law and common sense.

Students without previous civics, political science, or law classes might find the law section of the course more challenging than the ethics component. Law is precise; one wrong word can change the meaning of a case. Studying and understanding law requires reading and briefing court cases, memorizing legal tests, then applying them to real situations.

In my conversations with both media law and media ethics colleagues, there is notable disagreement about course formats and methods. Some argue that a combined course requires a simplistic narrative approach lacking substantial treatment of key US Supreme Court cases or neglecting areas, such as antitrust in media ownership. Media ethicists I talk to, particularly those advocating a strong theoretical approach in an applied ethics course, might complain that a combined course easily invites a case-study approach, which lacks a sufficient foundation in theory.

I have used the second option—the legal and ethical aspects of select topics and mass media professions. For the media law portion, we discuss the First Amendment along with significant areas of laws and regulation, including libel, privacy, obscenity and indecency, commercial speech, copyright, and access. In applying these concepts to the major media professions, we examine legal issues unique to print, digital and visual journalism, cable and broadcast television, the internet and social media, public relations, and advertising.

In the media ethics sections, we explore the differences between ethics and morals, ethical philosophies and theoretical foundations, establishing personal ethical identities, conflicts of personal and professional ethics, and ethical decision-making tools. While blending the traditional case study approach with a theoretical foundation for justifiable decision-making, we examine major ethical issues in the mass media professions mentioned above.

Rather than present a detailed ethical analysis of these cases, I only offer the basic facts and sample ethical questions, as a springboard to discussion. Instead of giving answers that students can recite back to professors, this approach challenges students to engage in their own creative, critical thinking about ethical issues, problems, and solutions. Taking that independent path, they make ethical decisions that they can justify and act upon and do not simply give the response they think the professor will like.

## WHY IS THIS COURSE IMPORTANT?

One of a combined course professor's objectives, not usually included on the syllabus, must be convincing students that a First Amendment education and ethical reasoning are crucial for their personal and professional development. Some higher-educational institutions include the need for their graduates to become "skilled ethical decision makers." Departments and colleges specializing in preparing students for mass media careers, both undergraduate and graduate, also cite the necessity of ethical training in their required curriculum. That demand for ethical competency also carries into the professional world. For example, in the 2017 Commission on Public Relations Education Report on Undergraduate Education

PR professionals placed ethics third, after writing and communication, as a crucial skill in the field, and stated that "new professionals" did not measure up to the industry's ethical expectations.[3]

The need for a rigorous First Amendment education goes beyond our future mass media practitioners avoiding costly litigation. Erick Ugland of Marquette University argued for "an increased emphasis on media law and policy courses and initiatives" to promote and increase public political advocacy for media policy issues. Among his rationale and strategies, Ugland included enhancing the protection of "expressive agency," fostering "political participation," and being involved in debates over "pressing constitutional and media policy issues."[4]

A combined course should include a history of our nation's free expression and significant free speech cases protecting that right, especially when threatened. A 2022 *New York Times* editorial, which included national polling, examined the growing threat to our First Amendment freedom of speech by stating: "For all the tolerance and enlightenment that modern society claims, Americans are losing hold of a fundamental right as citizens of a free country; the right to speak their minds and voice their opinions in public without fear of being shamed or shunned."[5]

The Accrediting Council for Education in Journalism and Mass Communication requires media law and ethics courses. ACEJMC lists 12 "specialized values and competencies" which may be required by mass media professions "irrespective of their particular specializations." At the top of the list is the need for a First Amendment education, stating that students must "understand and apply the principles and laws of freedom of speech and press, for the United States, as well as receive instruction in and understand the range of systems of freedom of expression around the world, including the right to dissent, to monitor and criticize power, and to assemble and petition for redress of grievances." An understanding of professional ethical principles is listed sixth: "Demonstrate an understanding of professional ethical principles and work ethically in pursuit of truth, accuracy, fairness, and diversity."

## WHAT A COMBINED COURSE SHOULD COVER

Here are the course objectives or "student learning outcomes" listed on my combined course syllabus.

### Think Critically about Existing American Media Law and Ethics

While some students might believe in an absolute First Amendment, others might call for limited government censorship to avoid "fake news."

Discussing alternative press models, such as government-owned and -controlled news media, could enhance their appreciation of our press and speech freedoms.

## Assess the Applicability of Existing Media Law and Ethics to New Media

Should obscenity rationales for print media developed by the Supreme Court in 1973 be applied to today's "new media"? By the time Congress or individual states pass laws to protect web privacy while accommodating the commercial needs of internet service providers, the laws are outdated by new technology.

## Be Able to Recognize Legal or Ethical Trouble

A combined course does not create media law attorneys or media ethicists. Instead, the law and ethics sections alert students to "red flags" regarding possible legal and ethical problems in their chosen professions.

## Appreciate How Developing Issues and Court Decisions Affect Professional Communicators

The news media provide many relevant legal and ethical examples to enhance class discussions of select issues and convince students of their relevance to our democratic freedoms. Did the Supreme Court make the right decision about a foul-mouth cheerleader's off-campus social media speech rights? The Court also set the test for incitement to lawless action which has been applied to defendants in criminal trials resulting from the January 6, 2021, storming of the US Capitol. Upcoming challenges to FCC regulations regarding web access (net neutrality versus reasonable management) could affect not only web access prices but also future media practices. And on the ethical side, every so often, a journalist is exposed as a plagiarist.

## Develop a System of Ethics Applied to Mass Communication

While I might be criticized for contradicting myself, I tell my students that I cannot teach them ethics. We will discuss theories, justification models, and decision-making tools, and then apply them to media ethical dilemmas. But they must discover their own ethical identity, which will evolve during their professional and personal lives.

## Discuss the Convergence and Conflict Between Ethics and Law

Law is what we *must* do; ethics is what we *should* do. The legislatures create laws; the courts interpret them; and the executive branch enforces them. But in ethics, who decides the "should"—the government, public, professional groups, companies, or individuals? For example, you are a reporter in a small town where a young girl has been abducted by a stranger. The community—the family, police, public, volunteers, and media—rallies to help bring the child home safely. Unless there are solid leads and new information, however, public awareness can fade along with media interest, despite visual events, such as holding candlelight vigils, passing out flyers, and hanging yellow ribbons. The family, meanwhile, opens their home and lives to the media to keep their child's story and photograph in the news.

As a parent, your editor understands the family's desperation and is anxious to keep the story alive. The editor sends you back to the neighborhood for a second-week story on local sentiments. Although insisting on anonymity, a reluctant neighbor confides that his daughter takes a swimming class with the missing girl and reports seeing bruises on her thighs. Other neighbors agree about hearing loud arguments and breaking dishes coming from the abducted child's home.

The local police confirm that they are investigating allegations of child abuse and domestic violence without further comments. Legally, you can write that story with verification that the police are investigating. From an ethical perspective, *should* you write that story? The family is experiencing enough, so why intensify their pain with such a story? Or do you have a duty to seek and report the truth?

## Engage as a Citizen

After reading Ugland's article, I adopted this outcome to motivate students to participate in our democracy as informed citizens and safeguard our First Amendment freedoms.

### TEACHING TIPS

While serving as teaching chair for AEJMC's Media Ethics Division, I wrote an article about how mass communication doctoral candidates were prepared for their teaching careers.[6] Only two programs offered any courses in teaching methods. As a result, we teach as we were taught—often a lecture with or without PowerPoint slides. While helpful, the slides should not be the primary focus of student attention. As one colleague suggested, "They are like a dance partner. Don't let them lead you." Or as a student wrote about my combined course on a professor-rating website, "Just download the PowerPoint slides and take a snooze."

With our students becoming more hesitant to participate in class discussions, the Socratic method can be more challenging than ever. During my doctoral studies at the University of Minnesota, I sat at the feet of a master of that method, Joel Samaha, for five criminal justice courses (my dissertation focused on the media's coverage of crime victims). While stressing that you can't force students to voice their ideas, he emphasized that careful questioning could motivate even the shiest student to participate. "It's not your first question that's the most important," he told me. "It's your second and third to help them think critically—like 'would you say that . . . ?'"

Some sample introductory ethical questions could be "Are you an ethical person?" or "Are you a moral person?"—then have the individual students justify their choices. For a preliminary First Amendment discussion, use relevant questions posed in the annual report on the state of the First Amendment by the Freedom Forum.[7]

Experimenting with other teaching tools, such as role-plays, will dramatize a professional ethical issue after the performing students discuss the problems in small groups. Show video clips from media-related movies or television shows, then apply ethical tools or justification models (e.g., Potter Box, SAD Formula, Doing Ethics) to the ethical issues posed. Although dated, I suggest short scenes from two classic films: *Absence of Malice* (Sally Field's character reporting a private person's abortion) and *Broadcast News* (William Hurt's character faking tears during a news piece cutaway). Borrowing from law school courses, have the students "argue" a case before a mock Supreme Court. After they read a landmark case, divide the class in half. One side argues for the petitioner, the other for the respondent. After the court rules (either you or a student panel), the sides switch and reargue the case.

## SAMPLE WRITTEN ASSIGNMENTS

Here are three suggested written assignments that cover media law and ethics both separately and together.

### Ethical Case Studies

In order to help develop ethical decision-making skills, students submit two two-page case analysis studies applying ethical theories, values, principles, and decision-making tools to two different case studies available in textbooks, web resources, video clips, or real-life events. Discuss sample case studies and resource materials when giving the assignment.

**Case Briefs**

Being able to succinctly brief court decisions can be an essential tool for understanding case law and its application to real situations. Students research and write two-page briefs for two selected cases. First, everyone briefs the landmark libel case *New York Times v. Sullivan*, for in-class discussion. For the second brief, students select a case from a provided list of other landmark media law cases. Sample briefs and resource materials should be presented in class.

**Position Paper**

With many issues involving media law and ethics, there will be at least two conflicting sides to the debate. To help students appreciate these conflicts involving free speech and mass media, they select a controversial topic in media ethics or law and write a four- to five-page position paper defending one side of the issue debate. Provide some suggested (not required) topics, such as flag burning, war media coverage, journalists' privilege, online privacy, or advertising of vice products.

## NOTES

1. A survey of the websites for 430 colleges and universities listed in the Association for Education in Journalism and Mass Communication 2011 directory indicated that 229 programs offer separate courses in media law and ethics (55 of those only offer media law, 23 only offer media ethics); 148 programs offer a combined media law and ethics course; and 7 offer both combined and separate courses; 13 websites did not list course information. The early stages of an updated survey based on the 2014 AEJMC directory (the last one issued) covered 36 schools (18 separate, 12 combined, six not listed).

2. "Designing and Teaching the Combined Law and Ethics Course," 105th Annual Conference, Association in Journalism and Mass Communication, Detroit, Michigan, August 4, 2022.

3. Marlene S. Neill, "Public Relations Professionals Identify Ethical Issues, Essential Competencies and Deficiencies," *Journal of Media Ethics* 36, no. 1 (2021): 51–67.

4. Erik Ugland, "Expanding Media Law and Policy Education: Confronting Power, Defining Freedom, Awakening Participation," *Communication Law and Policy* 24, no. 2 (2019): 271–306.

5. "Free Speech is Under Threat," *New York Times*, March 20, 2022, "Sunday Review," SR 4–5.

6. Jack Breslin, "Help! Some Advice for New Professors Who Find They Can't Teach," *Ethical News*, newsletter of the AEJMC Media Ethics Division, Spring 2006, 2.

7. Freedom Forum, "The First Amendment: Where America Stands," https://survey.freedomforum.org/.

# 8

# Ethics in Introductory Reporting Courses

Lee Wilkins, University of Missouri and Wayne State University

Teaching an introductory reporting class can be one of the most rewarding and challenging assignments. Introductory reporting requires students to learn a breadth of material, master some equipment, and learn about a campus or civil community. The research on teaching and learning here is clear: The more cognitive tasks introduced, the more likely students are to flub things they really do know how to do—like write in complete sentences—because they have become overwhelmed with other tasks—like AP style. But beginners make a lot of progress, rewarding for students and teachers alike.

The challenge is that students enter the course with distinct expectations. Suppose the program in which you are teaching requires all students to take introductory reporting (which may also be called media writing or information collection). In that case, your students may divide themselves into distinct groups. The first may be those students who envision themselves as majoring in news, and they will be positively invested in the class. Strategic communication majors, however, may enroll because the class is required and may view the course only as something to be survived.

Ethics can help you bridge this divide. Both news reporting and strategic communication demand accuracy—the first ethical step toward truth-telling. Both also demand thorough information collection. That accuracy and information collection requirement can be highlighted in many ways.

## GETTING STARTED

Many professors start by asking students to pair up and interview each other about why they are taking the class and what they expect from it. The students "write up" their interviews as brief profiles and then exchange their stories. The story subject evaluates what has been written, including completeness and accuracy. This is done through conversation. After that conversation, the students revise their initial stories based on colleague feedback. Only the revised story is turned in to the professor—to be graded or not. These profiles provide a great introduction to students at the beginning of the term as well as allow an instructor to gauge skill levels.

There are multiple goals for this assignment, but perhaps the most important is to give the student some sense of what it is like to be written about by someone they do not know well—a necessary introduction to the power of the media and some humility about exercising it. Humility is a building block of ethical thinking. It also allows students to talk to each other about what is accurate and what is not, what is complete, and what lacks detail and context. Finally, it allows an instructor to set baseline expectations early: names with proper spelling, addresses, age, pertinent background, accurate direct quotes, and paraphrasing are nonnegotiable. Getting these things wrong almost always hurts someone and destroys professional credibility.

### Connecting Accuracy and Truth

That discussion may actually come during the class period after the initial writing assignment, and it allows you to take questions about the distinctions between direct quotation and paraphrasing, what implications there are for capturing what the interview subject meant as opposed to the words that were spoken, and why it is so important to be accurate. You may also want students to bring in examples of news stories and advertisements they think are inaccurate or incomplete—and it may surprise you how they define accuracy when asked to apply it in the real world. (I require the students who aim for strategic communication careers to bring in news stories and the students who see themselves as future journalists to bring in ads or public relations releases.) This discussion may allow you to focus on the distinctions between accuracy and truth.

Telling the truth is not merely a matter of moral character. Learning what is true and how to detect truth is difficult and will continue to be so throughout a professional career.[1] Having students bring in current examples will also save you from the temptation of trying to teach this lesson through telling "war stories." Although you may have a distinguished professional career, to the students, you are "the professor" and they may see you as having crossed to the dark side of *teaching* rather than *doing*.

During the first weeks of class, creating assignments where getting the facts right (for broadcast students this may include nat sound or some video) increases the complexity of what the students are asked to do—and the potential for mistakes. At some point during this early part of the semester, introduce an exercise where an accurate paraphrase or quotation by a human source will result in a story that is incomplete at best or misleading at worst.

Some examples could include "he said/ she said" stories where the weight of the evidence is not equal but students may be tempted to write as if it is. (For potential case studies, examine books at the end of this chapter.) Ask students to bring to class examples of stories where they think this has happened. Require at least one of those examples to employ a potentially misleading visual image, for example, television coverage of the 2023 deluge in Monterey County,[2] which gave the impression that the entire state of California is under water when, in fact, large portions are still suffering significant drought.

Distinguishing between accuracy, completeness, and truth—the ethics lesson—is something that may not surface in these words until the middle of the term. The fact that technology has given us fake news, deep fakes, and now artificial intelligence-as-author will only broaden this discussion. If the ethics lesson you convey in your beginning reporting class is that telling the truth is the baseline for superior professional performance and that learning the truth and conveying it accurately is *hard*, you will have laid a foundation for ethical thinking for subsequent courses and a professional career.

## Information Collection from Human Sources

Today's students are described by some as reluctant reporters. They are happy to interview sources via email or even text; in-person interaction, however, is scary and many students will dodge the in-person-with-a-stranger approach in favor of relatives, roommates, or friends. Breaking this twenty-first-century habit can be difficult.

It's also difficult for students to focus on the interviewing process, especially if they are working on a deadline or struggling with tasks as varied as note-taking or utilizing new gear. For this reason, students should be given assignments that ask them to focus on the interviewing process itself. One such assignment is asking a student to interview someone they do not know about doing something. The "something" can be as simple as sewing a button on a jacket, as complex as glass blowing, or as unpredictable as reading to a group of 5-year-olds.

The parameters are important: the student must spend at least 30 minutes and as much as an hour watching the actual task. The student must allow time for interviewing the subject after the task is complete, and the interview must be recorded. The result is not a news story but an interview report that provides basic information on content, direct quotes that could be used for news reporting, and a self-critique of how the experience went. This includes but is not limited to: did I ask all the follow-up questions, did I leave major questions unanswered, did the subject explain what they were doing and why, what sort of visual images might work as part of the story, and did I get and follow up on anecdotes?

None of these questions are, in and of themselves, ethically focused, but they all speak to the notion of context and to developing a relationship with a source that allows for additional interviews when the student discovers—which often happens—that there is key information they have failed to obtain. I also tell students that one reason that broadcasters—radio or television—are often good interviewers is that they must listen to their own interviews as part of the reporting/editing process and, as a result, learn from their mistakes.

**Transparency**

After this initial interviewing assignment, students should read Metzler's "Creative Interviewing"[3] or a similar book, outlining the stages of the interviewing process. Emphasize that students need to introduce themselves with their real name, professional affiliation, the goal of the interview, and explain how long the interview will take. This is the beginning of a discussion of transparency with students. I tell my students that they haven't done a good interview if they can't tell me the eye color of their sources. Obtaining this bit of information requires eye contact and listening. It is the beginning of building rapport and trust with a subject.

Rapport and trust have a home in ethics, as well as in human relations—but the goal remains excellent professional performance. Determined, ethical interviewers get better stories. Two films illustrate this: *Spotlight*,[4] about the *Boston Globe*'s reporting of the pedophile priest scandal, and *She Said*,[5] about the *New York Times*' reporting of the Harvey Weinstein sexual assault allegations. Both provide viewers with a clinic on how to get subjects to open up about extremely difficult subjects. If you want to provide students with a lesson about how sources attempt to skirt journalists' questions, Crash Davis' instructions to major league rookie Ebby Calvin "Nuke" LaLoosh on how to respond to reporters' questions in the film *Bull Durham*[6] provides an excellent—and hilarious—rendition of every cliché good sports journalists know to avoid.

These films, as well as the interviewing assignments themselves, will allow you to introduce concepts such as on- and off-the-record, and the ethical and professional implications of making promises to sources that can become difficult to keep. Cleaning up quotes by correcting bad grammar, or deleting long pauses or repetitious phrases such as "you know," may also become the focus of the discussion. It is important to note that in contemporary newsrooms, where journalists are expected to file sound and images as well as written stories, the options for "cleaning up" quotes are limited, even if the individual journalist thinks it is desirable. If your standard remains "truth and accuracy," you will find that students will be inclined to paraphrase more, and since most journalists are better writers than the people they are interviewing, better stories will be the result. Broadcasters will need encouragement to provide something beyond a sound bite; again, accuracy in context provides an ethical standard that almost always results in superior professional work.

**Multiple Sources**

Interviewing assignments can be coupled with reporting assignments, but midway through the class, it is important to begin requiring students to develop multisource stories. Sources will begin to contradict one another, and students will need to learn how to handle differing opinions and, potentially, different facts. They will also need to learn an appropriate amount of skepticism when confronted with strongly held opinions. Opinions must be supported by fact, by truth in context, and not merely confirm preexisting beliefs. A journalist waits to be convinced by fact. A strategic communications professional acknowledges that facts supporting a call to action or some element of consumer behavior are almost always more successful in the long term.

The second assignment, which is among the last of the semester, is a full-blown personality profile of a newsmaker the student does not know. While public officials are often a first choice, strategic communication majors can select local business owners, restaurant staff—including the cooks—makers of various persuasions, etc. For this assignment, the student is required to interview a minimum of three people before interviewing the focus of the profile.

This second interview-based assignment is a complex one. It demands multiple sources, and it requires that students background themselves from something other than the web or social media. It also requires deciding on a focus from a lot of information, and it takes time and scheduling, especially when sources don't keep appointments. Getting others to talk about someone else requires transparency of purpose. The in-depth profile is as much an exercise in journalistic problem-solving as it is a straight-on reporting assignment.

## THINKING ABOUT HARM

Students are reluctant reporters for another reason: Many are afraid of offending someone with what they report. This unwillingness to do what they perceive as harming others will lead to all sorts of issues. My favorite is a strategic communication major in my reporting class who told me and her classmates that she wanted to go into advertising because she didn't want to invade the privacy of her sources the way she thought reporters did. (This in the era of strategic communication as targeted marketing—which has been referred to as surveillance capitalism. But no matter how misplaced, it is a perception that many students have about the journalistic process.)

Some good examples of how journalists balance the harm to sources versus harm to the body politic can be pulled from *Spotlight*. The film includes scenes balancing the harm of reporting very private acts with the benefits for the Boston community in knowing that pedophiles were among the Roman Catholic clergy. The foundational principle here is truth-telling, so students can envision how professionals justify their actions and help others understand them. What students need to grapple with is not only the concept of harm but also how harm may and may not be justified.

Students should also confront the harm done by not reporting something. For example, the Associated Press' recent decision[7] to no longer report names and other identifying information for those arrested for minor crimes constituted a major shift in journalistic routines. The reasons for this change are complex, but they certainly include an acknowledgment that arrest does not constitute a conviction, and most newspapers, broadcast stations, and even websites seldom follow up the arrest with stories about how the case itself is resolved.

There is also the issue of who gets arrested. Police departments are often required to report the ethnicity and age of those who are stopped for traffic violations. How should an ethical journalist report the arrest of someone who blows through a school zone at 90 mph as compared to the possession of a small amount of marijuana? What is the news here? What does the community need to know? Is there a pattern of arrests or convictions that reveals something about the institutions that constitute the US criminal justice system? In this instance, I want students to understand that the rules of style can have an ethical base and that they do have an ethical impact. Whether or not they believe the issue has been correctly resolved is something that will not be answered in your class, but, you do want students to know that the issue exists.

## TWENTY-FIRST-CENTURY TWISTS

As you know—and as your students will quickly find out—university administrations are not always tolerant of student journalists or their news outlets. Sources can take advantage of the information a journalist is required to provide to "talk back" in a variety of ways. Some are relatively inconsequential. But I have had students who have been threatened by sources (I'll tell your professor/dean/university president) and have been the focus of emails that are cruel and disturbing. I've been threatened that way myself.

Even in the basic skills courses, you will model what your students can expect from what we loosely call "the system." In this new world, sometimes it means sending students out in teams. It can mean substituting video conferencing for in-person interaction. It may also mean sending students to areas in their community with which they are unfamiliar, or to institutions with which they would prefer not to deal. In my graduate-level beginning reporting class, I had a student from Bulgaria to whom I had assigned the police beat. I expected the student to go to the police station and three weeks in, he still had not gone. As a frustrated editor, I asked why this otherwise bright and diligent student had failed this essential task, only to be told that, in Bulgaria, when you go to the police station, there is a good chance you will not come out. My solution, we went together—more than once.

The best editors I had in my professional career were those who were as concerned about professional growth as they were about getting the story. They gave advice; they listened. They backed me up when I needed it and guided me through the shame of having to write retractions. They were not always patient, and sometimes corrections were too public. But, my best editors (and colleagues, deans, and university administrators) respected the role of journalism and of teaching and tried to understand my approach. When I couldn't help my students, I tried to find resources on campus that could. My editors acknowledged my autonomy and dignity. How I was treated is how I try to treat my students. This, too, is a lesson in ethics.

## RESOURCES

Bok, S. 1978. *Lying: Moral Choice in Public and Private Life*. New York: Pantheon.
Metzler, K. 1997. *Creative Interviewing: The Writer's Guide to Gathering Information by Asking Questions*. New York: Prentice Hall.
Painter, C., and Wilkins, L. 2021. *Entertaining Ethics: Lessons in Media Ethics from Popular Culture*. New York: Rowman & Littlefield.

## CASE STUDY COMPILATIONS

Christians, C. G., Fackler, M., Richardson, K. B., and Kreshel, P. 2020. *Media Ethics: Cases and Moral Reasoning*, 11th edition. New York: Routledge.
Peck, L. A., and Real, G. S. 2016. *Media Ethics at Work: True Stories from Young Professionals*, 2nd edition. New York: CQ Press.
Wilkins, L., Painter, C., and Patterson, P. 2022. *Media Ethics: Issues and Cases*, 10th edition. New York: Rowman & Littlefield.

## NOTES

1. Sissela Bok, *Lying: Moral Choice in Public and Private Life* (Hassocks: Harvester, 1978).
2. "Update: Monterey County Levee Breach Prompts Evacuations, Water Rescues in Pajaro," CBS News, CBS Interactive, March 12, 2023, https://www.cbsnews.com/sanfrancisco/news/levee-breach-pajaro-river-evacuations-monterey-county-san-ardo/.
3. Ken Metzler, *Creative Interviewing* (Englewood Cliffs, NJ: Prentice-Hall, 1977).
4. *Spotlight*, IMDb, November 20, 2015, https://www.imdb.com/title/tt1895587/.
5. *She Said*, IMDb, November 18, 2022, https://www.imdb.com/title/tt14807308/?ref_=fn_al_tt_1.
6. "Bull Durham—Cliches," YouTube, November 3, 2008, https://www.youtube.com/watch?v=KeVca9MwDX8.
7. David Bauder, "AP Says It Will No Longer Name Suspects in Minor Crimes," AP NEWS, Associated Press, June 15, 2021, https://apnews.com/article/crime-technology-df0a7cd66590d9cb29ed1526ec03b58f.

# 9

# Ethics in Photography and Visuals

Alex Scott, University of Iowa

It is likely our students have swiped and scrolled through hundreds of images before a day's lectures have commenced. They have perhaps created photos themselves and circulated them to friends, family members—even strangers. A swarm of new mobile apps invites us to participate in the economy of the visual, and we spend increasingly more time in a virtual world of images. With ease, people can use the same platforms to share lighthearted memes as they can to circulate news images depicting grief and suffering.[1] The ubiquity and commonplace nature of these visual behaviors obscures the degree to which we are active participants in a visual news ecosystem with the capacity to create, share, circulate, and reframe the meaning of images.[2] If visual ethics are "the dynamic process through which we determine how best to create, disseminate, and use image-based stimuli,"[3] then visual ethics don't just apply to professional visual journalists. They apply to all of us.

Visual communication is a wide-ranging and diverse set of social practices, and one of the biggest challenges when teaching visual ethics is to define the scope of the curriculum. Visual ethics not only implies multiple modes of communication—photography, video, cartoons, graphic design—but it also refers to intersecting industries with multiple roles in society. Each medium possesses unique properties, such as the analogical quality and indexicality of photographs,[4] which must be explicated to meaningfully debate moral behavior. To complicate the matter further, teaching visual ethics in the context of journalism education can put normative aspirations at odds with the vocational realities of news work.

Rarely can a full course be dedicated to this topic, which requires imagination and creativity on the instructor's part.

This chapter seeks to address some of these issues and has three main objectives:

1. Delineate the field of visual ethics and provide some ideas about how to define the scope of your courses.
2. Provide alternatives to survey-style formats with active exercises to increase engagement.
3. Reorient ethical discussions from *them* "the media" to *us*, the active producers and mediators of meaning in a networked society.

I'll be focusing the discussion on photojournalism and photojournalism production courses, but I hope these ideas can easily be applied to broader media ethics courses, video journalism and documentary filmmaking, graphic design, and hybrid courses.

## PRIMARY CHALLENGES: FOCUS, FRAMEWORKS, AND ISSUES

The storytelling modality (e.g., video, photo, graphic design) and course type (e.g., skills-based production, seminar, lecture) are the primary factors that will influence the scope of your curriculum. With the proliferation of journalism/strategic communication hybrid courses, and journalism education's trend toward "multimedia," the task can be daunting. It is vital to think through the course's position in the context of the requirements and offerings of your institution. A department-wide skills and concept mapping initiative at the University of Iowa has allowed me to integrate ethics into multiple levels of production courses with some level of precision. As visual departments become smaller, and universities rely more on a rotating roster of adjunct faculty, it can be difficult to identify gaps and build in levels of complexity that also reduce redundancy.

Paul Lester[5] defined five areas of ethical concern with regard to images:

- victims of violence;
- rights to privacy;
- subject, image, and context manipulations;
- persuasion; and
- stereotyping

I've found this classification to be helpful when outlining the curriculum for a visual class, and to provide pathways to integrate visuals into every module of a broader media ethics course. For instance, persuasion and stereotyping are of great concern to strategic communication, much less than subject and image manipulation. Staging and digital manipulation issues are paramount to photojournalism practice and can be emphasized in introductory and intermediate-level courses.

I also think that the categories of victims of violence and rights to privacy are key areas of concern where a focus on images can help evolve the notion of them (the media) to us (active participants) in the networked news system. As a visual scholar, it is not surprising that I would advocate for integrating visuals into every lesson on media ethics, but images and visual practices are clear and accessible ways to problematize the notions of truth, objectivity, and responsibility in journalism practice.

If there is no dedicated or required media ethics course in your institution, time might be best spent instilling the theoretical tools of ethical deliberation. The Systematic Ethical Analysis[6] model is a great resource, detailing how to analyze many issues unique to visual production through a variety of frameworks. A basic understanding of common ethical frameworks—absolutist, golden rule, utilitarian—as proposed in Ken Kobre's influential *Photojournalism: The Professionals' Approach*[7] can be supplemented with duty ethics[8] and the ethics of care,[9] to diversify philosophical traditions and promote inclusion. *Ethics of Photojournalism in the Digital Age*[10] is an invaluable resource that lays out the ethics of photojournalism history and advocates for duty ethics in the digital mediascape. With this foundation in place, courses can be designed to activate moral deliberation, empower diverse voices, and balance normative aspirations with pragmatic realities.

If there is already a dedicated course on media ethics that prioritizes outlining prevailing frameworks and philosophies, more time and effort can be spent on specific issues that would arise in daily news work. I integrate ethics discussions into my modules by using Newton's division of ethics of process and ethics of meaning.[11] Ethics of process are a key component of journalism production courses, covering issues like staging, permission and informed consent, photographing public and private figures, and digital manipulation. Before my students leave the classroom to engage with the community, we run through exercises and discussions based on those topics.

During digital darkroom days, we discuss digital manipulation as we learn to crop, tone, and edit our images. Meaning ethics—such as representation, stereotyping, and publishing images of suffering—are topics I save for critiques when students have finished assignments. I've found that this method can better connect our discussions with their own work and experiences, allowing students to reflect on their practices and grapple with the tough decisions that come with editing and publication. While this approach allows ethical deliberation to be foregrounded in our practices, it can be difficult to find the time to contextualize the discussions within the history of photojournalism.

## SEEKING ACTIVE ENGAGEMENT: DEBATE, REFLECTION, AND CARE

As many instructors in this book have cautioned, teaching ethics must move beyond the recitation of "best practices" that equate to a set of pre-distilled heuristics for students to navigate their craft. This reproduces a status quo that has privileged certain voices in the industry and does little to prepare students for the unforeseen challenges of globalized, hybrid, and fragmented media systems. If the goal of teaching media ethics is to instill frameworks for critical thinking and provide space for moral deliberation, our courses should be designed to cultivate these through active and experiential learning.

When I was in graduate school at the University of Missouri, two of my seminars held structured debates by splitting the class into two teams and charging them with defending a position. Each one of these experiences has stayed with me for nearly a decade, albeit for very different reasons. In one course, our class was debating magazine representations—entertainment media—and the spirited debate extended beyond the classroom out to the café across the street. It inspired a level of critical and active consumption of media that I had not yet integrated into my daily routine. The other course debated the value of news images from the Iraq War. Though the conversation was of specific interest to me, I remained relatively silent as a group of students—assured in their position of these images as military-industrial propaganda by exploitative vultures—monopolized the conversation and used mockery to silence dissenting opinions. The atmosphere was combative and uncomfortable, but worse still, the nuance and complexity of these image-making practices were left uninterrogated. These experiences profoundly influenced my use of structured debate as a pedagogical tool. I have found that a modified debate structure is quite useful for exploring process ethics when the question becomes "Where is the line?" I have divided the class into two teams, each tasked with constructing a for or against argument for the issue at hand. Each team presents the argument and can respond to the others. Rather than attempting to win, or persuade, the goal is to delineate the nuance of the issue and promote continued engagement outside of the classroom.

I've found that the process of staging scenes or photographing staged "photo ops" is an excellent starting point to activate students' moral deliberation and develop mutual respect in class. Photojournalism communities have always encouraged staging in certain areas (e.g., environmental portraits) and deplored it in others. The paradox of staging allows students to explore many strains of thought, such as transparency and trust with audiences and the influence of events solely through a photographer's presence. I've structured the modified debate in three rounds, using images with varying levels of complexity. My most recent course started with a low-stakes example, an environmental portrait where boxers were demonstrating sparring techniques for the camera. Next, we moved on to a more difficult example: covers of *National Geographic* by Steve McCurry that are purported to be intricately staged scenes, including the famed "Afghan Girl." Finally, we end with "The Afronauts" by Magnum photographer Cristina de Middel,[12] which uses elaborately staged scenes to tell a nonfiction story about the unsuccessful Zambian space program in the 1960s. The overarching goal is to explore the complicated relationship between images and truth and to encourage students' own discovery and ethical formation. This format is also well suited for other process ethics issues such as exploring the nuance of digital manipulation or the debate surrounding informed consent[13] and asking permission from photographic subjects.

## STEREOTYPES AND CIRCULATION

Stereotyping, or conventionalized representation, is an ethical issue of interest to all visual classes regardless of focus, medium, or industry. I've found stereotypes to be more easily deconstructed in fictional media, foremost because of their overt and embellished nature but also because of the creative control that does not presuppose a level of truth. In photojournalism, I prefer to use the term "conventional representation," as in visual strategies (vantage point, lighting design choices, choice of moment, visual symbolism) that are consistently employed to photograph certain people in certain ways. Stereotypes are sets of widely shared cultural expectations, so they often seem innocent and plausible on the surface, especially when photojournalists defend their images as truthful. This requires some students to be sensitized to identifying stereotypical news imagery by looking at patterns of representation and listening to their reception by diverse audiences.

One approach I've found that enlightens students about the responsibility of representation is to bring the discussion into mundane visual practices. Rather than asking for students to give examples of news stereotypes, I ask students to think of a time that an image of themselves was posted online and circulated that represented them in an unfair, reductive, or distorted way. If students are active on social media, I'll encourage them to view their tagged images to identify patterns and try to imagine what others would think they knew about them based on the collection of images. The goal is to emphasize the responsibility of representing others and to begin a discussion on collaborative visual practices. This assignment also allows students to understand the reductive qualities of photography, especially how images flatten lived experience into a two-dimensional moment.

**Images of Suffering**

When the rich topic of visual ethics is condensed into one week's module or a single class period, images of suffering—death, grief, tragedy—are often singled out and presented more or less as a survey of horror. The ethics of publishing graphic images is an incredibly important topic, but perhaps more than any other ethical issue, the effects are profoundly personal. Before beginning any discussion on images of suffering, I like to contextualize the conversation by explaining three important concepts: the responsibility of spectatorship,[14] useful knowledge, and the notion of proper distance.[15, 16]

I first explain the responsibility of spectatorship derived from Azoulay[17] and Hariman and Lucaites[18] as ethics for the audience. When confronting images of suffering, audiences can passively consume them with a morbid curiosity or they can recognize the humanity in the people depicted and use the experience to inform their civic actions. There is a choice. Yet that choice is influenced by the context, form, and history of the image. In light of this, I discuss *useful knowledge* as a way of presenting images of suffering with the context necessary for audiences to understand the causes and explore potential remedies. Proper distance is a similar concept, but it is focused on a moral middle ground of representation, one that does not exploit the suffering of others, yet doesn't shy away or turn a blind eye to injustice and atrocity. The first concept justifies the discussion, the latter two allow the conversation to have a normative bent.

A canon of sorts has been constructed of graphic imagery buoyed by the controversy that surrounded their publication. Images with vexed appellations such as Richard Drew's "The Falling Man," Nick Ut's "Napalm Girl," and Kevin Carter's "The Vulture and the Little Girl" are joined by more recent examples such as the image of 2-year-old Alan Kurdi's body washed up on a Turkish beach, the assassination of Russian diplomat Andrei Karlov, and images of the war in Ukraine. I was shown some of these images in high school, undergraduate classes, and graduate school and, unfortunately, in my early courses as an instructor, reproduced the same surveys that usually end with, "What do you think?" This is an inadequate approach, as it does nothing to entice students to grapple with the ethical conundrums at hand or highlight their position as active participants in image dissemination. Even more troubling is that the survey approach often presupposes a homogenous American study body that is distanced from experiences of suffering. While I was teaching at the International Center of Photography, I once saw an international student in the hallway, sitting out of class because graphic images were being displayed from their home country. Great care should be taken to forewarn students of the images and ensure that they know they can leave the discussion without penalty if they feel overwhelmed.

One approach I picked up recently is the one-minute essay, a simple reflection exercise, where students have 60 seconds to write out their thoughts on a note card. It is commonly used as an assessment at the end of a lesson, but I have started to use this as a way for students to build confidence in classroom discussions. I use the exercise to precede a conversation about the ethics of publishing one or a small number of these images, and I instruct students to share their opinions on if an image's content and context could be considered useful information communicated at a proper distance. From this point, we can immerse ourselves in the discussion of bearing witness to history, expand into conversations of the perspectives from which these stories are told, and ask ourselves what we can do with this information to try to fight against injustice. The one-minute essay in its original iteration is also a useful tool for inclusive learning. The exercise can be implemented as an anonymous submission at the end of class to allow students to reflect on how these images made them feel.

Some scholars debate the utility of showing these images, but often this argument contains an unstated premise about the authorship of these images: They were made by outsiders to exploit suffering for profit. There are many examples historical and contemporary that counter this argument. I think about the photograph of the body of Emmett Till, and how his mother pushed to have the image published to evidence the horror and ensure no one could deny the injustice.[19] Therese Frare's image of David Kirby was published with the support of the family to destigmatize AIDS in the 1990s.[20] I don't believe there are any tidy answers to the ethics of publishing images of suffering, and no image of suffering can be compared to another from a separate context. These images have a high potential to disturb and cause emotional reactions, so they must be presented with the utmost care. Prefacing these conversations with Azoulay's ontology of the image[21]—a mass-mediated political or personal encounter with another—can mitigate our voyeuristic and apathetic potentials and instill a renewed purpose for image viewing, production, and image circulation.

## CONCLUDING THOUGHTS

Teaching visual ethics is a rich, complex topic that could easily fill out an entire course at the undergraduate and graduate levels. Our world and our communication practices are increasingly visual, and the unique properties of images require special attention. The main goal of this chapter is to provide some useful strategies for outlining your curriculum and engaging students, but the larger goal is to reorient visual ethics for modern media behaviors and possibilities. Students are simultaneously the producer, the publisher, and the audience—interacting with varied and overlapping genres of images. Connecting legacy media's ethical issues with more quotidian visual practices can emphasize this fact and empower students to bring fresh perspectives to the newsroom.

## NOTES

1. Nicholas Mirzoeff, *An Introduction to Visual Culture* (London: Routledge, 2009), 1.

2. Julianne H. Newton, "Photojournalism Ethics," in *The Routledge Handbook of Mass Media Ethics*, edited by Lee Wilkins and Clifford G. Christians (New York: Routledge, 2020), 119, https://doi.org/10.4324/9781315545929-9.

3. Paul Messaris and Linus Abraham, "The Role of Images in Framing News Stories," in *Framing Public Life: Perspectives on Media and Our Understanding of the Social World*, edited by Stephen D. Reese, Oscar H. Gandy Jr., and August E. Grant (Mahwah, NJ: Lawrence Erlbaum, 2003), 215–26.

4. Paul Martin Lester, Stephanie A. Martin, and Martin Smith-Rodden, *Visual Ethics: A Guide for Photographers, Journalists, and Filmmakers* (New York: Routledge, 2018), 7–11.

5. Ibid.

6. Ibid.

7. Kenneth Kobre, *Photojournalism: The Professionals' Approach*, 7th edition (New York: Routledge, 2017).

8. Clifford G. Christians, "Utilitarianism in Media Ethics and Its Discontents," *Journal of Mass Media Ethics* 22, no. 2–3 (2007): 113–31, https://doi.org/10.1080/08900520701315640.

9. Meenakshi Gigi Durham, "Resignifying Alan Kurdi: News Photographs, Memes, and the Ethics of Embodied Vulnerability," *Critical Studies in Media Communication* 35, no. 3 (2018): 240–58.

10. Miguel F. Santos Silva and Scott A. Eldridge, *The Ethics of Photojournalism in the Digital Age* (Abingdon, Oxon: Routledge, 2020).

11. Newton, "Photojournalism Ethics," 115–32.

12. Cristina de Middel, "The Afronauts," Cristina de Middel, accessed April 17, 2023, http://www.lademiddel.com/the-afronauts-1.html.

13. "Toolkit for Lens-Based Workers," Photo Bill of Rights, accessed March 5, 2023, https://www.photobillofrights.com/toolkit-for-lens-based-workers.

14. Robert Hariman and John Louis Lucaites, *The Public Image: Photography and Civic Spectatorship* (Chicago: University of Chicago Press, 2016).

15. Carrie A. Rentschler, "Witnessing: US Citizenship and the Vicarious Experience of Suffering," *Media, Culture & Society* 26, no. 2 (2004): 300, https://doi.org/10.1177/0163443704041180.

16. Roger Silverstone, *Media and Morality: On the Rise of the Mediapolis* (Cambridge: Polity, 2007).

17. Ariella Azoulay, *The Civil Contract of Photography* (New York: Zone Books, 2008).

18. Hariman and Lucaites, *The Public Image*.

19. *TIME* Photo, "The Photo That Changed America's Civil Rights Movement," *TIME*, July 10, 2016, https://time.com/4399793/emmett-till-civil-rights-photography/.

20. Ben Cosgrove, "World AIDS Day: The Photo That Changed the Face of AIDS," *LIFE*, January 15, 2020, https://www.life.com/history/behind-the-picture-the-photo-that-changed-the-face-of-aids/.

21. Azoulay, *The Civil Contract of Photography*.

# 10

# Public Relations Ethics Education in Advanced Courses

Katie R. Place, Quinnipiac University, and
Xiaochen Angela Zhang, University of Oklahoma

Ethics is considered a core competency in public relations education and has received considerable scholarly attention and pedagogical development for the past decade. In 2018, the Commission on Public Relations Education (CPRE) called for ethics to be a standalone required course and integrated as a topic into all public relations classes.[1] A 2022 CPRE spotlight report stated that ethical decision-making; codes of ethics; global ethics; corporate social responsibility; diversity, equity, and inclusion (DEI) ethics; and crisis communication ethics remain high priority topics of public relations ethics instruction. The commission recommended, however, that critical thinking and ethics, ethical decision-making, courage and confidence when addressing ethical issues, navigating misinformation, ethical listening, global ethics, and DEI ethics receive continued development and attention.[2]

Despite CPRE's call for public relations ethics to be taught as a standalone course, recent research has found that most communications and public relations programs do not yet have a dedicated ethics course. Instead, ethics instruction remains integrated into more generalized media ethics or law and ethics courses.[3] Recent research has also suggested that advanced public relations ethics courses utilize different pedagogical approaches and topics, including case studies, experiential learning, and client work, so that students may better engage, analyze, and grapple with ethical situations.[4] [5] Ethics taught in standalone public relations courses offer more comprehensive coverage of ethical topics, including other codes of ethics beyond the Public Relations Society of America (PRSA) code of ethics, classical philosophies, decision-making models, and other perspectives on ethics.[6] More advanced coverage of ethical topics integrating experiential learning are more likely to meet industry expectations of public relations graduates in terms of ethical competency such as development of moral courage and personal ethics.[7]

Little scholarship, unfortunately, has sought to review the philosophies and pedagogical techniques incorporated into teaching advanced undergraduate public relations ethics. Therefore, the purpose of this chapter is to survey common content divisions for teaching advanced public relations ethics, examine the pedagogical techniques for delivering content, and discuss implications and recommendations for its instruction.

## KNOWLEDGE: PUBLIC RELATIONS ETHICS COURSE CONTENT

For public relations students to gain an advanced understanding of moral philosophies and their practical applications, they must gain not only knowledge (K), but also skills (S) and abilities (A), referred to as KSAs.[8] To support students' knowledge (K), core content areas of instruction should address foundational moral philosophies, professional and business ethics applications, codes of ethics, decision-making models, and emerging or current trends. We recommend assigning a grouping of readings or content that includes a) a foundational reading, such as a book chapter on a particular concept, and then b) contemporary case studies, relevant peer-reviewed journal articles, or recent news or trade press articles. Core areas of ethics content for public relations are discussed in more depth below.

### Moral Philosophies

Foundational moral philosophies appropriate for teaching of advanced public relations include virtue ethics (e.g., Aristotle), deontology (e.g., Kant), utilitarianism (e.g., Mill, Bentham), ethics of justice (e.g., Rawls), and feminist or care ethics (e.g., Gilligan). At the beginning of the course and before learning about each new moral philosophy, we recommend reviewing key moral philosophy and ethics terminology with students. For example, when students learn about deontology, they may need to familiarize themselves with such interchangeable terminology as "Kantianism," "Kantian ethics," "categorical imperative," "duty ethics," or "rationalism."

### Macro-Level Applications

Additionally, course content featuring macro-level applications or practices will advance students' knowledge of moral philosophies and their applications to the wider business and public relations profession.

Content may include modules and readings dedicated to the subtopics of business ethics, corporate social responsibility, the role of the ethical conscience or guardian, ethical leadership, cultivating an ethical business culture, ethical management of media and business, or fostering excellence across public relations practice.

## Codes of Ethics

Students will benefit from knowledge of professional codes of ethics, their applications, and their enforcement. Codes of ethics particularly relevant to advanced public relations education include Public Relations Society of America (PRSA) Code of Ethics, the Arthur Page Principles, the IABC Code of Ethics, the Institute for Advertising Ethics Code, and the Society of Professional Journalists' Code of Ethics. Relevant resources are also available via Arthur Page Center online teaching modules or the PRSA.org ethics web page. On the PRSA.org ethics site, students can learn about the PRSA Code of Ethics professional values and code provisions, read position papers by PRSA Board of Ethics and Professional Standards (BEPS) white papers, and read recent PRSA ethics advisories on emerging issues.

## Decision-Making Models

In addition to foundational moral philosophies and their business applications, knowledge of ethical decision-making models (which draw upon such moral philosophies or principles) is important. Relevant decision-making models include Sissela Bok's decision-making model,[9] Ralph B. Potter Jr.'s "Potter Box,"[10] and the TARES test.[11] Bok's model relies heavily on the moral principles of empathy and social trust.[12] The Potter Box asks individuals to draw upon their knowledge of moral philosophies, which may include virtue ethics, utilitarian ethics, deontological ethics, or care or agape ethics, among others.[13] The TARES test guides practitioners to consider moral decisions, reflect upon their practices, or enact their moral conscience using the five principles of truthfulness, authenticity, respect, equity, and social responsibility.[14]

## Global, Cultural, and Diversity-Centered Ethics

To fulfill CPRE's calls for more global, critical, and inclusive understandings,[15] advanced course content should seek to advance students' knowledge of global ethics; diversity, equity, and inclusion (DEI) ethics; critical and cultural approaches to ethics; and ethics of evolving technologies. Course content regarding ethics of social and mobile media, data management, artificial intelligence, and other new communication technologies in public relations contexts is also necessary for students to understand the evolving nature of the industry. For these topics, a variety of resources are available to students including the Institute for Public Relations' Digital Media Research Center, Pew Research Center's "Internet & Technology" resources, PRSA Silver Anvil Case Studies, and the Arthur Page Center Training Module on "Digital Ethics."

## SKILLS AND ABILITIES: PEDAGOGICAL APPROACHES TO PUBLIC RELATIONS ETHICS

In addition to knowledge (K), it is important for educators to offer students means to also hone their skills (S) and abilities (A) of advanced ethics concepts. A variety of pedagogical approaches including online or in-class discussions, case studies, assessments and exams, reflection opportunities, role playing, service learning, and client work are available to facilitate students' understanding, retention, and practical application of material.[16,17,18] Generally, educators should break out instruction of concepts into separate class periods or modules, pair instruction of philosophies or concepts with historic or contemporary case studies, and offer students sufficient time to discuss, reflect upon, or apply concepts. Common pedagogical approaches to advanced public relations ethics instruction are reviewed below.

### Discussions and In-Class Engagement

Discussions and in-class dialogue facilitate the teaching of ethics, offering students dedicated spaces to make meaning of or grapple with concepts. Discussion-based teaching techniques include weekly discussion board posts, leading or co-facilitating in-class discussions, or simply actively participating in class discussions. Educators may wish to assign daily, weekly, or biweekly discussion board posts or prompts to complete prior to class. Keeping up with weekly ethics readings and discussion posts helps students to actively prepare for and participate in robust discussion and dialogue with their peers in class. Discussion posts or prompts completed prior to class also offer an opportunity for educators to review students' understanding of concepts prior to class to identify which topics may need more clarity or attention.

### Case Study Analysis or Critique

Case study readings and case analyses or critiques offer excellent opportunities for students to apply their knowledge and ethical decision-making skills to real-world situations. Case studies can be easily incorporated into course readings or online course modules to supplement instruction of moral philosophies, ethical values, codes of ethics, or decision-making modules. Commonly utilized case study collections pertaining to public relations ethics include Wilkins, Painter, and Patterson's textbook *Media Ethics: Issues and Cases*;[19] Brunner and Hickerson's textbook *Cases in Public Relations: Translating Ethics Into Action*;[20] Arthur W. Page Case Study Competition cases; and Public Relations Society of America Silver Anvil winning cases. Reading current news articles or trade publications can also provide robust opportunities for students to apply their knowledge of concepts to the profession.

### Assessments and Exams

In addition to discussions and case studies, traditional assessments such as quizzes, exams, or essay tests are necessary to gauge students' abilities to recall and apply concepts. Quizzes are appropriate tools to help students periodically assess their knowledge of concepts or course readings. Exams or long-form essays offer an opportunity to more comprehensively assess students' understanding of concepts, knowledge of ethical principles and practices, and ability to compare or apply concepts. Directions should clearly identify which concepts or readings are being assessed and how students should complete the assessment.

### Codes of Ethics Assignments

Codes of ethics critiques and personal/professional codes of ethics development assignments pose an additional pedagogical technique.[21] In such assignments, students can read and compare the PRSA, IABC, and SPJ Codes of Ethics and provide analysis, critique, and recommendations for code amendments. Additionally, students can be asked to read a variety of organizations' codes of ethics, and then draft a hypothetical public relations or communications code of ethics for an organization that lacks a code.

### Reflection Opportunities

Reflection is a particularly important component of ethical thinking and moral awareness. Therefore, advanced public relations ethics courses would benefit from a variety of reflection-based pedagogical techniques. Discussing personal ethics and virtues while reflecting on one's own experiences can help facilitate students' understanding of their personal moral views,[22] engagement in critical thinking, and development of tactics to enact moral courage.[23] Studies have found that university students often draw from personal experiences and moral exemplars in the surrounding environment to develop their own moral reasoning and to establish their moral foundation. College classrooms serve as a perfect vehicle to deliver moral foundations through pedagogy that help students to "a) reflect on moral values and the roles they play in students' holistic lives, b) engage in dialogue about virtues and moral foundation concepts, and c) have opportunities to explore and refine their moral awareness."[24] For example, students could engage in in-class dialogues or reflection essays to connect abstract moral concepts with their real-life experiences, especially those related to their public relations career goals after service learning or experiential learning opportunities.[25]

## IMPLICATIONS AND RECOMMENDATIONS

Teaching of advanced public relations ethics requires a proper balance of instruction of knowledge, skills, and abilities (KSAs)[26] regarding moral philosophies and professional applications, decision-making models, and codes of ethics. Codes of ethics and decision-making models such as the Potter Box require individuals to have a working knowledge of ethical principles and moral philosophies, so it is especially important for public relations ethics pedagogy to begin first with an introduction to core moral philosophies such as deontology, utilitarianism, justice, care/agape ethics, and virtue ethics. It usually takes students some time to digest these abstract concepts, and it is recommended that public relations ethics courses dedicate sufficient time covering these philosophies, especially via applying the philosophical principles on real-life cases or contemporary events.

A gap still exists between what is taught in advanced public relations courses and what the 2022 CPRE report recommends.[27] More emphasis should be placed on ethics instruction centered on critical thinking and personal virtue/moral development, which are skills essential for public relations practitioners to navigate misinformation and to develop courage and confidence when addressing ethical issues.[28,29] Increased use of contemporary case analyses and experiential or service learning will better equip students to identify, assess, and address common ethical dilemmas in sophisticated ways.

Advanced public relations ethics instruction must better emphasize KSAs regarding global ethics; diversity, equity, and inclusion (DEI) ethics; critical and cultural approaches to ethics education; and ethics of evolving technologies. Pedagogical tools such as reflection exercises and critique opportunities could help students more fully grasp and apply concepts. For example, students can be asked to critique and offer revisions to a company policy or an organizational code of ethics, or to write a reflection on a current event in which an organization has behaved unethically with regard to DEI or global ethics. For evolving technologies and social media, educators could address KSAs by assigning a research essay about the ethics of an emerging technological advancement, having students review and critique an organization's social media or data management ethics policies, or having students draft their own hypothetical social media or data management guidelines for an organization.

There are few textbooks dedicated specifically to the teaching of public relations ethics. The lack of specific texts may exist because public relations ethics is rarely taught as a standalone course and is often taught in combination with media law, advertising ethics, or journalism ethics, thus shrinking the market or call for such books. The lack of dedicated texts may leave some instructors utilizing a mixture of readings and news articles from various textbooks, websites, academic journals, or trade press outlets. Regardless, more public relations profession-centered texts and resources with consistency of content involving moral philosophies, ethical applications to practice, as well as critical approaches that consider DEI, intercultural, and global nuances in the public relations profession are needed.

Ultimately, public relations ethics educators have a complex duty and balance to ensure advanced ethics instruction adequately prepares students to enter a fast-paced and constantly evolving industry. They need to a) inform students about moral philosophies or professional values, b) introduce professional examples and cases where those philosophies or values are applied or infringed upon, and c) ensure that students are capable of making ethical decisions in complex environments. To juggle these considerations, it is important for public relations ethics educators to adopt a mix of KSA-based learning content, a variety of pedagogical techniques, and a mix of moral philosophies to undergird them.

## NOTES

1. Commission on Public Relations Education, "Fast Forward: Foundations and Future State. Educators and Practitioners," 2018, http://www.commissionpred.org/commission-reports/fast-forward-foundations-future-state-educators-practitioners.

2. Commission on Public Relations Education, "Fast Forward: Updates on Public Relations Education: Spotlight Series," 2022, http://www.commissionpred.org/wp-content/uploads/2022/10/CPRE-Ethics-Spotlight-Report-2022-10.29.pdf.

3. Teri Del Rosso, Matthew J. Haught, and Kimberly S. Marks Malone, "Accreditation, Curriculum, and Ethics: Exploring the Public Relations Education Landscape," *Journal of Public Relations Education* 12 (2020).

4. Ibid.

5. Katie R. Place, "Exploring Ethics and Client Work in Public Relations Education," *Journalism & Mass Communication Educator* 73, no. 4: (2018): 421–38.

6. Marlene S. Neill, "Ethics Education."

7. Marlene S. Neill, "Public Relations Professionals Identify Ethical Issues, Essential Competencies and Deficiencies," *Journal of Media Ethics* 36, no. 1 (2021): 51–67.

8. Institute for Public Relations, "The 2017 IPR and PRSA Report: KSAs and Characteristics of Entry-Level PR Professionals," 2017, https://instituteforpr.org/2017-ipr-prsa-report-ksas-characteristics-entry-level-pr-professionals/.

9. Sissela Bok, *Lying: Moral Choice in Public and Private Life*, 2nd edition (New York: Vintage, 1999).

10. Clifford G. Christians, Mark Fackler, Kathy Brittain Richardson, and Peggy Kreshel, *Media Ethics: Cases and Moral Reasoning*, 11th edition (New York: Routledge, 2020).

11. Sherry Baker and David L. Martinson, "The TARES Test: Five Principles for Ethical Persuasion," *Journal of Mass Media Ethics* 16, nos. 2–3 (2001): 148–75.

12. David W. Guth, "The Bok Model," 2011, https://dguth-journalism.ku.edu/BokModel.pdf.

13. Christians et al., *Media Ethics*.

14. Baker and Martinson, "The TARES Test."

15. Commission on Public Relations Education, "Fast Forward."

16. Neill, "Ethics Education."

17. Del Rosso et al., "Accreditation."

18. Place, "Exploring Ethics."

19. Lee Wilkins, Chad Painter, and Philip Patterson, *Media Ethics: Issues and Cases* (Lanham, MD: Rowman & Littlefield, 2021).

20. Brigitta R. Brunner and Corey A. Hickerson, eds., *Cases in Public Relations: Translating Ethics into Action* (New York: Oxford University Press, 2019).

21. Katie R. Place and Xiaochen Angela Zhang, "Understanding Public Relations Ethics Education in Advanced Courses: A Qualitative Thematic Analysis of Course Syllabi," Conference Paper, AEJMC, 2023.

22. Michael Lamb, Jonathan Brant, and Edward Brooks, "How Is Virtue Cultivated? Seven Strategies for Postgraduate Character Development," *Journal of Character Education* 17, no. 1 (2021): 81–108.

23. Commission on Public Relations Education, "Fast Forward."

24. David A. Craig, Katie R. Place, Erin Schauster, Patrick L. Plaisance, Michael Humphrey, Christopher Roberts, Ryan Thomas, Casey Yetter, and Jin Chen, "Moral Foundations in Life Narratives of Emerging Adults in Media-Related Fields," Conference Paper presented at AEJMC Conference to Media Ethics Division, 2021.

25. Place, "Exploring Ethics."

26. Institute for Public Relations, "The 2017 IPR and PRSA Report."

27. Place and Zhang, "Understanding Public Relations Ethics Education."

28. Neill, "Public Relations Professionals."

29. Place, "Exploring Ethics."

# 11

# Ethics in Broadcast News Classes

April Newton, Loyola University Maryland

In the early 2000s, when I was working as a news producer, an incarcerated man at a state prison took hostage a woman who worked at the facility. The incident lasted hours, with the region's news outlets all covering it live until the inmate was killed by a sharpshooter. The hostage later chose to tell the story of her experience to Eve (Tannery) Russo, a reporter from our station. Russo had been following the story for weeks after the initial incident when she was suddenly offered the opportunity to do an interview with the woman. Our station aired the emotional and important interview—but only one time. The managers recognized that her story was an important one for the public to know, especially accusations that security lapses at the prison put her and others in danger. The managers also recognized, however, that the potential trauma of broadcasting the interview was going to be significant and, to protect the woman, the interview never aired again.

Broadcast journalism faces the same ethical considerations as other platforms on which journalism is accessible, but there are several key concerns tied to the specific affordances of broadcasting. The sight and sound of someone telling their own story may be compelling, but it may also present serious ethical concerns about a person being revictimized by the initial broadcast and any subsequent transmission. Concerns shouldn't be reserved only for victims, of course, as the long shelf-life of audio and video, the popularity of both on social media, and the speed with which journalists can share raw video and audio all present unique ethical challenges for broadcasters. For many students in journalism courses, the ubiquitous nature of video is not something they question, so it is a good place to start ethics discussions, and an excellent lesson can take place as students head out to record their first interviews for use in broadcast journalism.

## REDUCING HARM TO SOURCES

Students in my classes often ask if they are required to tell a subject that the interview is "on the record." I start by telling them that ethical interviewing, particularly for broadcast, requires more intentional care than just explaining that it's on the record. The Society of Professional Journalists' Code of Ethics includes the imperative to "minimize harm," and specifically to "show compassion for those who may be affected by news coverage. Use heightened sensitivity when dealing with juveniles, victims of sex crimes, and sources or subjects who are inexperienced or unable to give consent. Consider cultural differences in approaches and treatment."[1] In "Why Should I Tell You?: A Guide to Less-Extractive Reporting," published by the Center for Journalism Ethics at the University of Wisconsin–Madison, Natalie Yahr compiled advice from reporters who often cover stories with people in marginalized communities like undocumented workers or previously incarcerated people.[2] The reporters said it was ethically crucial to make sure people know talking to a reporter can have an impact on their jobs, their status in the United States, or their freedom. In an article for National Public Radio's training guides exploring the ethics of interviewing, Emma Grazado recommends explaining in detail everything from the purpose of the interview, to how it will be conducted, to what part of the interview may make it on air.[3]

An important conversation is happening about extending similar care to all people who participate in news interviews, not just victims or the marginalized. Often described as going through a process of "informed consent," proponents suggest making sure an interview subject or source knows there could be consequences to doing an interview and discussing what the potential consequences might be. Some conversations have included leaving the door open for an interview subject to withdraw participation right up to the last minute.

Informed consent is an important point of entry for journalism students to weigh their competitive impulse to get a story against the care of other human beings. It serves also to remind students that someone may be a witness or a victim, or the perfect example of a certain experience, but that person is first and foremost a human being. Russo, the reporter who interviewed the woman held hostage in the prison many years ago said incremental, careful, accurate reporting eventually helped her get the interview with the victim.[4] When Russo and the woman sat down together, Russo knew it was a privilege to hear the woman's story in her own words:

I remember waiting and letting silence happen and letting her gather her thoughts and choose her words. It had taken so much to get to that moment, in terms of the reporting I had done but it was her story and she was crying and I thought, "I'm not going anywhere until she is done, even if I miss deadline and get fired, because she is giving me something so precious right now."[5]

In broadcasting, even a professional sports star is nearly as vulnerable as any "regular" person because video could end up changing the course of their lives. In 2003, NFL Hall of Famer Joe Namath was drunk at a professional football game and tried to kiss ESPN reporter Suzy Kolber during live coverage.[6] The incident illustrated the challenges women reporters face every day, bearing the brunt of sexism in the bro-ish culture of professional sports, but it's also a good example of the longevity a broadcast interview can have. Kolber ended the interview fairly quickly and later said her thought was, "Uh-oh, Joe is in trouble here, and let's get him out of it."[7] Namath wrote in his autobiography that the incident was life-changing and helped him examine his drinking.[8] It was also a moment that followed Namath; 20 years later there are more than two million views of just one of the many YouTube clips of the exchange.

## USING MATERIAL FROM OUTSIDE THE NEWSROOM

The propensity for people to record everything happening around them means newsrooms can now seek out and use material from events and angles taken by someone outside the newsroom. Video shot by teenage witness Darnella Frazier completely altered what the public understood about the 2020 murder of George Floyd by Minneapolis police. Video of the heroic and safe 2009 landing of a US Airways plane by pilot Chesley Sullenberger in New York's Hudson River was recorded by a tourist on a nearby ferry. In those and other high-profile cases, the videos end up being shown so often on television and on social media feeds that credit for their original "videographers" becomes lost. It is important to reinforce to students the necessity of giving proper credit for any material used in a broadcast that was not recorded by the newsroom, either through direct reference, particularly for radio, or with lower third graphics or bugs for video presentation. Credit is both a legal issue of copyright and also an issue of the ethical application of fair use exceptions. A vague understanding of either is where students often get into trouble.

I make it standard practice to share a set of tips prepared by the librarian at our school who acts as the copyright expert. Many universities and colleges have someone with similar expertise, and library websites may have a section devoted to such explanations. There is an excellent explanation, with good examples, available through the Stanford University

Library website, prepared by Richard Stim, under the heading "Fair Use," linked in the references section.

It is a good idea to remind students that journalists don't typically pay sources, as a matter of ethics, but it is important to make sure people are fairly compensated for their work. Many students are able to quickly screenshot material on a phone and share it via text and social media, and the popularity of memes that are based on existing videos and screenshots further cements the ubiquity of using material that already exists and is easily available online. It has been common, in my experience, for students to use maps, graphics, archival photos, and more, that they record or screengrab from online sources. We take time to go over getting permission to use what they find and to find out how to pay for using it when necessary, or more importantly, teaching students where to find ethical, free sources for their needs. The US Library of Congress, local historical societies, and some university archives often have abundant material that is available to the public, as do a number of government agencies and many nonprofits. For instance, the Centers for Disease Control and Prevention website has widgets, buttons, and graphics related to COVID-19 information and data that is available for public use, clearly marked, and easy to find online.

Another ethical concern about using material from outside a reporter's own newsroom is the blind trust that another reporter is correct. From time to time, a student will reference statistics from the *New York Times*, for example, that are actually statistics from a government agency or university research, included in a *New York Times* article they read as part of their research. When it happens, it's a great opportunity to help students understand that reporting is not the same as writing a term paper and their ethical obligation is to go to the original source for information they find online. If the student's story is inspired by reading about the latest jobs report in the *Baltimore Sun*, then the student must go to the report from the Department of Labor's Bureau of Labor Statistics, rather than quoting the *Baltimore Sun* article. For students, it's also a great opportunity to practice finding original information and a good reminder that they must be able to take responsibility for the information they include in their stories.

## DOING CONTEXT CORRECTLY

The struggle against misinformation is going to occupy newsrooms for the foreseeable future and an important tool in the fight is prioritizing care for context. In a post on "The Power of Context" by the Digital Resource Center from the Stony Brook Center for News Literacy, there is a wonderful definition to use in a classroom discussion:

Context: a set of facts about some event that happened today takes on more meaning, and accuracy even when the writer gives you context, such as the HISTORY that led to the event, COMPARISON to similar events, CONNECTION between these players and outside parties, and responsible PREDICTIONS of what comes next.[9]

It is entirely possible to provide some measure of context in the compressed reporting of day-to-day news for broadcast and it's important to train students that it is an ethical imperative with implications for the survival of a free press and democracy.

In placing context at the top of the list of ethical priorities for students, it can be helpful to start with what it means to use information out of context. Vanderbilt University psychology professor Lisa Fazio said that out-of-context photos are "a particularly potent form of misinformation."[10] While we hope reporters aren't purposely seeking to confuse their audience, the impact of shortcuts and sloppy reporting can't be undone very easily. Brendan Nyhan addressed the problem with reporters taking a quote out of context in a column breaking down the coverage of a widely reported story involving then-presidential candidate Mitt Romney in 2012. Writing in the *Columbia Journalism Review*, Nyhan closed by saying "News-starved political reporters have lost sight of the fact that their first responsibility is to lay out the facts for readers, not to summarize the spin."[11]

For many journalism students and, if we're being honest, long-time professionals, the issue of context arises because people simply don't know enough history. Take, for instance, the example of Christopher Columbus statues pulled down in the wake of George Floyd's murder and a reckoning over who is celebrated in the United States. In some communities, the destruction or removal of the statues was covered by reporters simply as acts of vandalism or protest, causing insult to Italian Americans and leading some people to feel like it was more lashing out by activists who didn't respect tradition.[12] The *Washington Post*, in one helpful article for use in the classroom, put the statues and Columbus' role in US history into a context that indicates Columbus was useful to different groups interested in developing a specific image, hence the statues, cities, and other memorials to his name across the country.[13] According to the reporters who wrote the article, most of those efforts ignored evidence of the atrocities and incompetence that marked Columbus' expeditions for the sake of a convenient rallying point. Further, the *Washington Post* article includes information about decades of anti-Columbus activism that indicate pulling down statues in 2020 was part of a long history of protest.

Context is also about simpler issues of using video or sounds correctly, whether in a context appropriate to a story or in context to the intention with which the video or audio was originally gathered. Again, thinking about the big picture will help students learn that if a popular, well-liked mayor is arrested for embezzlement, then it's important when telling the story to use both videos of the mayor's perp walk and video of the mayor being cheered at a rally by the people who voted for her.

## ETHICAL CONCERNS WHEN NEWS IS UGLY

Sometimes broadcast news involves visual and auditory information that is simply horrible. The videos of George Floyd's and Ahmaud Arbery's murders were essential to getting correct the facts about what happened to both men, particularly in the face of efforts to hide how events unfolded. Recordings of racist rants by store employees or elected officials, and violent treatment of Black and brown children by teachers and school employees have gone a long way toward illustrating and underscoring the continuous threats against people of color in the United States. There is, however, ample concern from psychologists about the long-term damage to audiences of color who are subjected to seeing the videos over and over as the stories are reported on for days and in some cases, years.[14] Some have also raised concerns about the way in which the videos carry an entertainment value, getting passed around on social media and resurfacing for years.[15]

There is a true ethical challenge in weighing how to tell stories of recorded acts of violence, bias, and hatred against the potential to further hurt members of marginalized communities, keeping in mind everything from reducing harm to sources to using material generated by someone outside the newsroom to developing context to using materials in the correct context. The classroom is an important place to open the challenge to students about how to treat stories where the evidence and confirmation lie in ugly recordings of events. The Radio Television Digital News Association's code of ethics reminds journalists to tell the hard stories with care, including the important point that "Shying away from difficult cases is not necessarily more ethical than taking on the challenge of reporting them. Leaving tough or sensitive stories to non-journalists can be a disservice to the public."[16] Ask students to consider decisions about what it means to show care for all the members of their community, especially when the truth is particularly unkind.

## NOTES

1. SPJ, "SPJ Code of Ethics—Society of Professional Journalists," Society of Professional Journalists—Improving and Protecting Journalism since 1909, September 6, 2014. http://spj.org/ethicscode.asp.

2. Natalie Yahr, "Why Should I Tell You?: A Guide to Less-Extractive Reporting," Center for Journalism Ethics (blog), n.d., University of Wisconsin–Madison, https://ethics.journalism.wisc.edu/why-should-i-tell-you-a-guide-to-less-extractive-reporting/.

3. Ibid.

4. April Newton, Eve (Tannery) Russo, personal interview, April 13, 2023.

5. Ibid.

6. "Namath Apologizes; Knight Goes on Tirade: [FINAL Edition]," *Washington Post*, December 24, 2003, D02, https://www.proquest.com/newspapers/namath-apologizes-knight-goes-on-tirade/docview/409558023/se-2.

7. "ESPN's Suzy Kolber Speaks About Joe Namath 'Kissing' Incident," American Sportscasters Online, n.d., http://www.americansportscastersonline.com/suzykolberjoenamath.html.

8. Cindy Boren, "Namath: Drunken Interview Saved Life," *Washington Post*, May 9, 2019, https://www.proquest.com/newspapers/namath-drunken-interview-saved-life/docview/2221579954/se-2.

9. "The Power of Context," Digital Resource Center: Center for News Literacy, Stony Brook University, https://digitalresource.center/content/power-context.

10. Lisa Fazio, "Out-of-Context Photos are a Powerful Low-Tech Form of Misinformation," The Conversation (blog), February 14, 2020, https://theconversation.com/out-of-context-photos-are-a-powerful-low-tech-form-of-misinformation-129959.

11. Brendan Nyhan, "The Out-of-Context Quote as Gaffe," *Columbia Journalism Review* (blog), Columbia Journalism School, January 17, 2012, https://archives.cjr.org/united_states_project/the_out-of-context_quote_as_ga.php.

12. Examples: Nicholas Pfosi, "Protestors Tear Down Christopher Columbus Statue in Saint Paul, Minnesota," Reuters News Service, June 10, 2020, https://www.reuters.com/article/us-minneapolis-police-saint-paul-statue/protesters-tear-down-christopher-columbus-statue-in-saint-paul-minnesota-idUSKBN23I04X.

Johnny Diaz, "Christopher Columbus Statues in Boston, Minnesota and Virginia Are Damaged," *New York Times*, June 10, 2020, https://www.nytimes.com/2020/06/10/us/christopher-columbus-statue-boston-richmond.html.

13. Youjin Shin, Nick Kirkpatrick, Catherine D'Ignazio, and Wonyoung So, "Columbus Monuments Are Coming Down, But He's Still Honored in 6,000 Places across the U.S. Here's Where," *Washington Post*, October 11, 2021.

14. Kenya Downs, "When Black Death Goes Viral, It Can Trigger PTSD-like Trauma," PBS *NewsHour*, National Public Radio, July 22, 2016.

15. Dahlia Lithwick, "Stop Playing Violent Videos of Black People's Deaths," *Slate*, April 26, 2021.

16. "Code of Ethics—RTDNA," Radio Television Digital News Association (RTDNA), June 11, 2015, https://www.rtdna.org/ethics.

# 12

# Ethics in Student Media
Nicole Kraft, The Ohio State University

It was the summer of 2020 and sparks from the flame surrounding George Floyd's death at the hands of Minneapolis police had blown onto our campus and set off a firestorm of civil unrest. Hundreds of students gathered on the steps of the university administration building, chanting and holding signs. Student government leaders gave moving speeches that brought roars from the crowd. They passed a megaphone around so speakers could be heard above the crowd; each identified themselves by name, major, and year in school. Although the academic year had already ended, members of the student media returned to campus to capture history as it unfolded, armed with recorders and cameras, notebooks, and laptops. They were joined together in a beautiful First Amendment dance—the right to protest and the right to a free press.

That dance ended, however, the moment a hand went up in front of a camera and the protestors demanded there be no recording of any faces, no publishing of any names, and no coverage of this event. Reporters said they would be using names, comments, and images to cover this important protest. They were threatened with a lawsuit and a promise to be reported to the university for misconduct. This is our home, said the protestors. Student media had no right to infringe. This is our home, the student media said. They had a right to cover any news that broke on campus.

Welcome to the world of the modern-day student journalist, where the convergence of coverage and ethics is intertwined every day of their academic and journalistic lives.

For many former journalists teaching journalism today, there was a clear and methodical pathway from our journalism education to a professional career. We started in student media, covering campus or sports, before moving on to a weekly publication or, if lucky, a small daily. After a couple of years, we moved up to a bigger daily, and then maybe bigger still. We moved forward, built our clip portfolio and resumes, and, maybe most importantly, made mistakes to learn from in order to be at our performing peak when we reach our career pinnacle.

That path has surely changed.

With the contraction of media at all levels, student journalism is no longer just a class or an extra-credit activity that is shared among handfuls of on-campus participants. Now it is the gateway, even the first step, into a professional-style journalism career, with online engagements that span the globe.[1] That means long-lasting ramifications for those who report and those who are reported upon. Similar to professional media, student media perform as watchdogs for the public that they serve, checking and balancing university administrators, faculty, student government, and other institutional authorities.[2]

This chapter is a guide to teaching ethical considerations to student journalists who are experiencing publication of their work that transcends campus boundaries and may be an entry-level position for future journalists. It is our job as instructors to ensure that an ethical net catches the students who may make mistakes born out of a lack of experience—mistakes that can ruin their lives and the lives of those they cover.

It is the job of student journalists to cover news on and around campus. Reporting on an urban campus the size of Ohio State is basically covering a midsized town. Beats for student journalists include politics and development, infrastructure and medicine, galleries and arts, dining, and student life. Our job as journalism faculty is to prepare student-journalists for any story that may need covering. The writing and reporting skills learned in their journalism courses are showcased in the student media, but so also the mistakes they make if their work is not built on a foundation of ethical decision-making.

Research shows that students do not engage with or apply ethics as much as they should in college classrooms but instead apply ethics by working in student-led newsrooms, and newsroom experiences influence student beliefs about ethical issues.[3] Ethical foundations are key to journalism at every level—and have a heavier weight of meaning when intertwined with academics. This includes plagiarism and fabrication, sins at every level of academia but even more so for our journalism friends who recognize the paths forged by Jayson Blair, Stephen Glass, Janet Cooke, and other infamous journalists.[4]

But the ethics we confront go even deeper and to a more foundational level of relationship-building among people who live, work, and socialize in the same small community. There is an inherent challenge to the world of student-journalism that tests reporters to be as fair as possible while continuing to be active members of the communities on which they report. The actions of the university president or board of trustees affect them the same as other students. Tuition hikes hit their wallets. That immersion provides access and insight, but it also requires systems and procedures to avoid even the appearance of impropriety.

That same university leadership on which student-journalists report to ensure accountability for actions and policies may also control their newsroom budgets. The quest for public records (which at our university has led student media to file two successful lawsuits against the university when that access was unfairly limited) must go through the same administrators that student-journalists rely on for information or comments for stories.[5] Such power imbalances and conflicts of interest, combined with student journalists' relative inexperience, are a recipe for a journalism environment riddled with ethical potholes.

Another challenge is that classroom activities cannot replace the real experience of practice, which means student-journalists are often facing the real consequences of their decisions for the first time while working in student media. Actions of students may significantly differ in situations when consequences are real.[6] A college campus is a unique community where journalists cannot help but intermingle with those they cover—from their classmates who star on a football team or are elected to student government, to the professors who grade them, to the administrators who lead the university and also might provide their funding. The principles that ground ethical decision-making remain a crucial element of journalism education.[7] As the Society of Professional Journalists' Code of Ethics[8] outlines, key ethical tenets for journalists include:

- Be Responsible.
- Be Fair.
- Be Honest.
- Be Accurate.
- Be Independent.
- Minimize Harm.
- Be Accountable.

Research shows that students who take courses in journalistic ethics are acquainted with these principles and their significance, but a significant percentage said they believe framed ethics present stricter principles than are required to do a reporting job and almost 20 percent said speed and exclusivity were more important than respecting the rules of ethics.[9]

As educators and journalists, we often shape journalistic education around the SPJ Code, but there are missing elements to that document, related specifically to the intertwining of the news industry and collegiate life. Among the key challenges are the need to be professional and transparent in our pursuit of coverage, to diversify voices in reporting, to serve the population inside and outside campus boundaries, and to ensure that fairness and accuracy shape all news coverage.

## CONFLICTS OF INTEREST

One of the most significant issues confronted by student journalists involves conflicts of interest, which can be inherent for student media covering the school they attend. Conflicts of interest in journalism arise in circumstances in which there is the appearance or guarantee that the judgment and performance of journalists might be influenced by outside interests they have that lie beyond their journalistic responsibilities.[10] Students want to rush Greek life, belong to groups, and cheer for athletic teams. Can they do those things and remain objective journalists? They want to write features on their friends, favorite professors, or the charitable dance marathon in which they take part every year. The question is whether their involvement in an activity forever skews their ability to be—or the perception that they are—impartial regarding coverage.

It's essential to guide student-journalists through disclosing potential conflicts of interest that may prevent them from being objective or may cause readers/viewers to question their ability to report objectively. Many news organizations have policies that limit or prohibit accepting gifts, getting involved in politics, and other situations that pose conflicts of interest in journalism.[11] That does not mean all stories with a conflict are off-limits. I taught a football player who, as a journalism major, wanted to profile a teammate with a compelling story that would likely not have been accessible to other journalism students—or professional reporters. But the conflict of the two being teammates was a barrier for our student-editors. The solution: reveal the conflict of interest to the reading public. Honesty allows news consumers to decide if it feels like a conflict or not. If there is a personal issue or unavoidable conflict of interest, real or perceived, in covering stories or participating in editorial decisions, revealing them to advisers and editors right away will allow reporters to work through the potential for coverage or participation.

Student-journalists must also recognize they are not part of the story. As much as they may support an event or cause, they must maintain journalistic independence and objectivity in reporting. This means, also, that they might be prevented from taking part in some collegiate experiences open to others, such as running for leadership of a group, belonging to a political student group, or even running for office in student government.

## SOURCING

Being fair and accurate when reporting stories starts with student media recognizing the need to identify themselves as a reporter anywhere and everywhere they encounter a source or potential source, and that would include classes, school facilities, or social situations. Considering all the places a student-journalist might encounter potential sources, and the fact most of those people are not experienced in being engaged in journalistic practice, transparency is the only way to walk an ethical pathway through campus. We also have extraordinary access to students through online directories, class environments, dorm life, and socializing. Exposing people when they have an expectation of privacy is unethical. Consider overhearing conversations in classes, dorms, libraries, or dining halls that could be used to augment coverage. Consider engaging in a class discussion where they learn something personal about a student-athlete or student-government representative—information to which they would not otherwise have access. We must help student-journalists find the line where coverage ends and life begins.

Many sources, especially students who are not savvy about media coverage, may not realize the long-lasting implications of the information they provide. Ensure sources are aware that the information they are providing can and will be disseminated beyond the boundaries of campus. The need to be aware of coverage of vulnerable populations—including but not limited to minors, international students for whom English is not their first language, students who may be intoxicated, and students who are in environments that make them susceptible to peer pressure—is key to maintaining ethical standards in working with sources.[12]

The unintended or undesirable consequences that may result from a story or interview in the near term and in the future for sources need to be considered when breaking news. Views held and actions taken in late teens and early 20s can have long-lasting ramifications in the age of Google, which means student media specifically must be aware when posting controversial viewpoints or compromising images that may have questionable news value. We also must confront the realities of unpublishing requests and the possibility that it might be ethical under certain circumstances to consider them.[13]

## COVERING THE COMMUNITY

Dignity and respect are vital to reporting fairly. If student-reporters are not trusted, their work means nothing. A key part of ethics for the student-journalist involves ensuring coverage serves all the people who comprise a college community. The people they cover are not just students—they are often residents of the campus community, as well. Be respectful of their personal space, which may overlap the academic environment. Words that live online have a long and everlasting reach. Establish content-neutral policies and apply them with fairness and a full explanation. Make sure your publication's policies regarding ethical decision-making are firmly established and based on sound theory and experience. Make it available as a public resource and also take the time to explain them to constituencies, including student, faculty, and staff populations.

There is no way to avoid bad things that will happen on campus, and we will be required to cover them. In just the last few years at Ohio State, we have had a student murdered on her way home from work, a rash of students who took their own lives jumping from campus parking structures, a terrorist attack that resulted in a student death (the attacker) and accompanying lockdown, allegations of sexual assaults by student-athletes, and the revelation that a campus doctor molested dozens of student-athletes over decades before taking his own life. That's not to mention the forced "retirements" of university presidents and football coaches, campus protests, and more. The ethical choices we make in covering these stories stay with students during their time in student media and beyond.

One spring break our campus editor sacrificed a week at the beach to cover the murder trial of a suspect who had abducted, raped, and shot a student in the head while on supervised release.[14] During a recent spring semester, the staff covered the rape trial of two former football players that resulted in an acquittal, but not before testimony about collaborative sexual practices that challenged their moral values.[15] In both instances, student-journalists credited their classes with providing the education they needed to report even under the most challenging of circumstances, through conversations in classes, guest speakers who shared their own reporting stories, live reporting simulations that take students out of their comfort zone, and follow-up dialogues when coverage gets tough. Mental health in reporting was even a specific focus.[16]

The majority of student-journalists want to be and act ethically. They have entered journalism not to take advantage of others but instead to serve their community fairly and accurately, in a quest for the truth that will make their population better informed. Yet the circumstances of an environment of student reporting ultimately make it open to some aspects of unethical framing due to the very space in which it takes place and the very people who do it. Taking the time to explain to young journalists why ethical considerations around conflicts and sources are significant when it comes to their immediate and future success is just as important as teaching the inverted pyramid or AP Style. It is, in truth, a foundation of journalism at its core—the ability to recognize and execute ethical behavior in every aspect of reporting at every level.

## NOTES

1. Stephen J. Ward, *Radical Media Ethics: A Global Approach* (Chichester, UK: John Wiley and Sons, 2015).

2. Terry L. Hapney, "Student Newspaper Governance on Public University Campuses in Ohio: Higher Education Administrators vs. Student Journalists" (doctoral dissertation, University of Dayton, 2012), retrieved from http://unr.idm.oclc.org/login?url=https://search-proquestcom.unr.idm.oclc.org/docview/1651232900?accountid=452.

3. David H. Weaver, Randal A. Beam, Bonnie J. Brownlee, Paul S. Voakes, and G. Cleveland Wilhoit, *The American Journalist in the 21st Century: U.S. News People at the Dawn of a New Millennium* (Mahwah, NJ: L. Erlbaum, 2007).

4. Mike Conway and Jacob Groshek, "Forgive Me Now, Fire Me Later: Mass Communication Students' Ethics Gap Concerning School and Journalism," *Communication Education* 58, no. 4 (2009): 461–82, https://doi.org/10.1080/03634520903095839.

5. Kaylee Harter, "Ohio State Found in Violation of Ohio Public Records Law," *Lantern*, September 13, 2019, https://www.thelantern.com/2019/09/ohio-state-found-in-violation-of-ohio-public-records-law/.

6. Dragana Pavlovic, "Education of Journalism Students and Their Perception of Journalistic Ethics," *Teaching, Learning and Teacher Education* 6, no. 1 (November 1, 2022): 59–72, first page, https://doi.org/https://doi.org/10.22190/FUTLTE220514004P.

7. Ann Auman, Susan Stos, and Elizabeth Burch, "Ethics Without Borders in a Digital Age," *Journalism & Mass Communication Educator* 75, no. 1 (2020): 9–15, https://doi.org/10.1177/1077695820901941.

8. SPJ, "SPJ Code of Ethics," Society of Professional Journalists, 2014, http://spj.org/ethicscode.asp.

9. Pavlovic, "Education of Journalism Students."

10. Sandra Borden and Michael Pritchard, "Conflict of Interest in Journalism," in *Conflict of Interest in the Professions*, edited by Michael Davis and Andrew Stark (New York: Oxford University Press, 2001), 73–91.

11. Ibid.

12. Michael Ryan, "Journalistic Ethics, Objectivity, Existential Journalism, Standpoint Epistemology, and Public Journalism," *Journal of Mass Media Ethics* 16, no. 1 (2001): 3–22, https://doi.org/10.1207/s15327728jmme1601_2.

13. Erin Gretzinger, "Lack of Industry Guidance on 'Unpublishing' Practices Leaves Student Journalists in the Dark," Center for Journalism Ethics, December 1, 2022, https://ethics.journalism.wisc.edu/2022/12/01/lack-of-industry-guidance-on-unpublishing-practices-leaves-student-journalists-in-the-dark/.

14. Lantern Staff, "Reagan Tokes Trial: Jury Recommends Golsby Get Life in Prison Without Parole," *Lantern*, March 21, 2018, https://www.thelantern.com/2018/03/reagan-tokes-trial-golsby.

15. Aubrey Wright, "Former Football Players Found Not Guilty of 2020 Rape and Kidnapping," *Lantern*, February 9, 2023, https://www.thelantern.com/2023/02/former-football-players-found-not-guilty-of-2020-rape-and-kidnapping.

16. Dart Center for Journalism & Trauma, "PTSD & Mental Health," Columbia Journalism School, https://dartcenter.org/topic/ptsd-mental-health.

# III

# ETHICS IN SPECIALIZED TOPICS

# 13

# Covering Law and Justice

Kathleen Bartzen Culver,
University of Wisconsin–Madison

When George Floyd was murdered by Minneapolis police officer Derek Chauvin on May 25, 2020, any reporter relying on the word of the Minneapolis Police Department would have—quite accurately—written that Floyd died "after a medical incident."

The statement issued by the department that day reported, "Officers were able to get the suspect into handcuffs and noted he appeared to be suffering medical distress. Officers called for an ambulance. He was transported to Hennepin County Medical Center by ambulance where he died a short time later."[1]

The statement is accurate. Floyd was handcuffed, and he suffered medical distress. What's missing is the context. Between the handcuffing and the distress came more than nine brutal minutes of Chauvin kneeling on Floyd's neck while he was restrained, including at least a full minute when Floyd was unconscious. Citizen video of the incident almost immediately went viral. Without it, routine news coverage would almost certainly have featured the police statement, which was technically accurate but missed the full context, making the statement wildly untruthful.

Cases like this make journalism classrooms a critical space to discuss how the common practices of covering law and justice, including deference to authoritative sources like police, can lead to untruthful and unethical news coverage. As an educator, you have an obligation to your students—and to the citizens they will eventually serve—to challenge news routines and encourage deeper and more inclusive reporting about criminal justice and public safety. Few of us have the luxury of dedicating a full semester to specialized reporting on law and justice, so let me offer three key lessons you might incorporate into any reporting class and some resources to support these ideas.

## DEFERENCE TO AUTHORITY

The Floyd case is just one example of how reporting can go wrong when we defer too easily to sources who are seen as authorities. Police and prosecutors have a justified position as important sources in criminal justice stories, but their voices should not dominate. Encourage students to seek out defense attorneys, victims, and advocates from across the spectrum of their reporting.

One useful case to explore with students is covering crimes related to substance-use disorders. I begin by acknowledging the likelihood that many people in the classroom have been affected by use and abuse of alcohol or other drugs among family or friends. Then we discuss that in the United States, we most often see substance-use disorders through the lens of crime—a man arrested on his fifth drunk driving charge or a woman convicted of child neglect after overdosing in a park. I then challenge the students: If your only sources were law enforcement authorities, your stories would frame substance-use disorders in criminal contexts. Think of someone in your life who has struggled with addiction. Is the word "criminal" the first one that comes to mind?

As an exercise, you can then turn to a local news site and find a story at the intersection of crime and substance abuse. Sadly, the search will not take long. Walk your students through an effort to generate one or two other angles to take on this story and generate source lists that move beyond authorities to people with lived experience and those advocating for other ways to address this social problem. One of the most important takeaways will be that covering individual crimes is, in itself, something to be skeptical about in reporting. But more on that in a bit.

## NAMING AND UNPUBLISHING

One of the most discussed issues in law and justice coverage is who to name and when. This often arises in cases involving children or sexual abuse and assault, but it matters in other contexts, as well. An important and long overdue conversation is unfolding in journalism today about how news coverage can exacerbate injustices. Research clearly demonstrates inequities in the criminal justice system tied to race, ethnicity, gender, socioeconomic status, and treatment of marginalized groups.

The question then becomes: Does news coverage double down on those injustices by amplifying them?

The Associated Press in 2021 released a new policy that it would no longer name people arrested for or charged with minor crimes because of the long-lasting effects of the coverage, such as people's ability to find jobs or housing.[2] This issue often lands in the newsrooms of student media, where editors face requests to unpublish stories about criminal activity on campus—from bar fights to sexual assault allegations.

One useful classroom exercise is a case study approach. The Center for Media Engagement at the University of Texas is an excellent resource, and their case on unpublishing is particularly compelling.[3] You could have students read through the case and work in small groups to cover the discussion questions. Or you could set up the activity with groups assigned to defend whether to unpublish or not. The Center for Journalism Ethics at the University of Wisconsin–Madison has more resources specifically aimed at student media that are worth assigning as class reading.[4]

## EPISODIC VERSUS THEMATIC COVERAGE

Among the thorniest ethics issues in all of journalism is the question of what to cover and how. Scholars highlight the difference between episodic coverage that emphasizes individual events or happenings and thematic coverage that sees the connective tissue between events and focuses coverage on the bigger picture. In short, think of it as the difference between covering one warehouse fire and examining all fires in a warehouse district over years and whether inspections or building codes are lacking. News coverage of the justice system is rightly criticized as too focused on episodic coverage. We cover a compelling child abuse trial but don't ask enough questions about systems in place to protect kids. We lead the 6 p.m. news with a sensational drunk driving arrest but do not dedicate a series to recovery from alcohol addiction.

This is, at heart, an ethics issue. I frame it to my students as the difference between micro and macro ethics. When I was a police and courts reporter, I strived to be ethical in my work. I sweated decisions about whether to name a crime victim. I argued for a move from reporting arrests to reporting only when a person was criminally charged. These were important questions, yet they were micro questions—the necessary but small matters of reporting. What I missed were the macro questions. I was a justice reporter at the height of the "war on drugs" and the dawn of mass incarceration in the United States. I did not ask the overarching questions about the systems I was reporting on and their massive effects on society. I needed to step away from the day-to-day coverage of arrests and trials and ask, "why are we doing this?"

An excellent exercise for students in this arena is a coverage audit. Assign them to a local TV outlet for two weeks. Have them audit stories that run. How many related to law and justice? When do they run in the newscast? What is the run time? Who are the sources featured? Are they episodic or thematic? During that same two weeks, have them read one story per day by The Marshall Project, the leading nonprofit journalism organization focused on criminal justice, https://www.themarshallproject.org/. The exercise will demonstrate to them with crystal clarity how different our systems look when we move from the day to day to the longer lens.

**NOTES**

1. John Elder, "Man Dies After Medical Incident During Police Interaction," Minneapolis Police Department, May 25, 2020, https://web.archive.org/web/20200526183652/https://www.insidempd.com/2020/05/26/man-dies-after-medical-incident-during-police-interaction/.

2. David Bauder, "AP Says It Will No Longer Name Suspects in Minor Crimes," Associated Press, June 15, 2021, https://apnews.com/article/crime-technology-df0a7cd66590d9cb29ed1526ec03b58f.

3. Deborah L. Dwyer, "Should Our Past Follow Us Forever Online?," Center for Media Engagement, University of Texas at Austin, December 13, 2021, https://mediaengagement.org/research/should-our-past-follow-us-forever-online/.

4. Erin Gretzinger, "Lack of Industry Guidance on 'Unpublishing' Practices Leaves Student Journalists in the Dark," Center for Journalism Ethics, December 1, 2022, https://ethics.journalism.wisc.edu/2022/12/01/lack-of-industry-guidance-on-unpublishing-practices-leaves-student-journalists-in-the-dark/.

# 14

# Data Ethics

Jasmine E. McNealy, University of Florida

For more than a decade, commenters have heralded the potential use of the voluminous troves of personal data in sectors like medicine, finance, criminal justice, and sports.[1] Training on these massive datasets would assist in making faster and more accurate diagnoses, limit risk in lending, mitigate human subjectivity in court proceedings, and help choose the best hitting lineup for our favorite baseball team.[2]

At the same time, we are aware of the fallacy of a utopian view of data. Algorithms trained on medical data place Black Americans lower on the transplant list or exclude them altogether. Banking algorithms trained on data disparately place loan applicants from certain zip codes in the high-risk category. Criminal justice algorithms amplify already entrenched racial prejudices in determining bail and sentencing.

But data are just data, right—neutral and unbiased?

These statements and others made about emerging technology that frame data and technology as disinterested and objective are inaccurate.[3] To understand why, it is important to have a working definition of the term "data." In this chapter, data are defined as a system of networked representations or observations.[4] Data are not solo points but snapshots or records of occurrences at specific times in the past, which are then connected to other snapshots or records of other happenings that occurred sometime in the past.

Data does not exist in a vacuum but rather in systems that shape their collection, use, and interpretations. These systems impact the attachments to data—the labels, categories, and meanings that data carry—and can be shaped by bias and prejudice. Most can recognize the harms connected with examples of failures in using data and datasets in high-stakes systems like criminal justice and health care. Even in lower-stakes sectors, including data use in media or communications professions, negative impacts occur. Journalism, advertising, and other organizations use data and data products for public-facing and organizational tasks. Many of these uses are legal. Often, these uses are attached to adverse effects on the people implicated by the data.

In the face of a lack of regulation, professional communicators must consider the ethical implications of data. This chapter aims to assist media students, educators, and professionals to critically examine the possible impacts of their collection, use, and storage of data. Data ethics, then, are critical considerations about how and whether data should be collected, used, and made available. These critical considerations include accuracy, fairness, and transparency, all of which fall under the broad term impact.

## ACCURACY

A common use of large-scale data by professional communicators is through data journalism,[5] which uses numerical evidence to tell a story. The goal of data journalism is to assist the public in understanding an issue, often with visuals and interactive, digital tools. The numerical evidence used to tell the stories can come through the aggregation and analysis of data from public and nonpublic sources.

Ethical issues around the use of this data can include questions about the accuracy of the data collected. Although data can come from public or government sources, this does not mean it is completely correct. The *Texas Tribune*, for example, published in 2013 the Prisoner Database, composed of data that came directly from the Texas Department of Criminal Justice about all the inmates in state custody. It then unpublished it for a period of time after receiving complaints from the family members of inmates that the data was inaccurate.[6] Many prisoners convicted of sexual assault were coded instead as having been convicted of "sexual assault of a child." When asked about the discrepancy in the data, a spokesperson for the TDCJ stated that the coding for assigned crimes was done by hand to match federal criminal codes. When a coder encountered a crime without direct federal code, the staff member entered "the closest match to the offense title"[7] and had not checked for accuracy. The miscoding, and the publishing of this inaccurate information, left inmates and their family members open to ridicule and possible danger. The *Tribune* removed the database until it was redesigned to remove federal criminal code designations.[8] The paper retired the database in 2020.[9]

## FAIRNESS

Fairness with data is typically defined as the collection, use, and analysis of data in a way that does not reinforce bias.[10] Bias exists and is a part of all data systems. Negative biases, however, can disparately and negatively impact communities and groups. In the United States, federal antidiscrimination laws exist to stop the negative effects of bias related to race, gender, and other identifiers within housing, employment, and other contexts. Even with these laws, organizations, including media organizations, have been found to discriminate using data.

Facebook came under fire, for example, for its creation of a tool that allowed advertisers using its platform to discriminate in targeting users.[11] The tool was powered by the many points of data Facebook collected on its users, like geography, race, gender, and political affiliation,[12] along with the interpretations of that data, to sell access to advertisers. Advertisers were able to more effectively target the people they considered to be the audience for their product or service.

On its face, a tool powered by personal data would seem like a great innovation, especially for small businesses that may not want to waste money on an ineffective campaign. But some advertisers used the tool to exclude groups of users based on racial identifiers. After significant negative attention, Facebook removed the multicultural affinity tool.[13] While a clear racial identifier might include "Asian American" or "Latino," proxy identifiers also exist that can provide predictive value for advertisers looking to reach specific racial or ethnic groups.[14] Instead of searching specifically for "Asian," an advertiser might target users mentioning terms like "pho," "K-pop," or "Bollywood." This kind of targeting can exclude a significant number of people from receiving information.

## TRANSPARENCY

Another major consideration in data ethics is transparency or an organization's openness to scrutiny. Transparency exists when an organization clearly details when and how it will collect, use, and make data available.[15] The goals of transparency include making people aware of how their personal data might be used and allowing the organization to be held accountable for practices that run contrary to its stated claims and public values. Conflicts about the lack of transparency often arise after an organization is found to have been collecting and using personal data in ways that go beyond the bounds of what is expected and accepted.

Crisis Text Line, an AI-driven mental health chatline, was found to have shared user data with a for-profit spinoff organization and was forced to make data use disclosures more conspicuous.[16] CTL is a nonprofit that uses data-driven technology to provide mental health services to those in crisis. To do this, CTL collects the text conversations with its users and allows its for-profit child organization, Loris.ai, to use portions of that data to create and advertise customer service systems. CTL claimed that the data had been anonymized and did not contain information that could identify users.

A significant issue with CTL was that it had collected what was thought to be one of the largest mental health datasets in the world.[17] This kind of data could provide insights into mental health and effective crisis communications, but even with the supposed anonymization, research has shown that it is not difficult for those in possession of data to trace back the disclosures in the data and reidentify users. Although CTL provided users with a 50-paragraph disclosure about usage and data collection, questions arose as to whether people in crisis are aware of how their data might have been collected and then used. Following the exposure of the data-sharing program with Loris.ai, CTL changed its privacy policy to provide clear details about how data might be collected and shared. It eventually decided to discontinue its data-sharing program and asked Loris.ai to delete any data that it had received.[18]

## THINKING CRITICALLY ABOUT DATA ETHICS

The three scenarios are but a few that demonstrate the media- and communications-related ethical dilemmas that can arise with the massive collection, use, and sharing of data. There are, of course, others reflecting the impact that individuals and organizations using data may have. These require critical considerations for all of those thinking of collecting and using data. Accuracy, fairness, and transparency are just a few of the factors that should be examined in data ethics. A probe of transparency, for instance, finds that this ethical consideration is also connected to areas like privacy and accountability, both of which are important subjects for scrutinizing data-use impacts on people and organizations.

Students, teachers, and professionals should endeavor to inspect the areas of importance for the project that they are creating. The scenarios above demonstrate the importance of these considerations in areas like media and communications, which have traditionally been deemed of lower risk than areas like health, criminal justice, and finance. No matter what the area, if there are impacts on people, they must be studied before the product is released.

## NOTES

1. danah boyd and Kate Crawford, "Critical Questions for Big Data," *Information, Communication & Society* 15, no. 5 (2012): 662–79, https://doi.org/10.1080/1369118X.2012.678878.

2. Cathy O'Neil, *Weapons of Math Destruction: How Big Data Increases Inequality and Threatens Democracy* (New York: Crown, 2016).

3. Langdon Winner, "Do Artifacts Have Politics?," *Daedalus* 109, no. 1 (1980): 121–36.

4. Jasmine E McNealy, "An Ecological Approach to Data Governance," *Notre Dame Journal of Ethics, Law and Public Policy* (forthcoming 2023), https://papers.ssrn.com/sol3/papers.cfm?abstract_id=4164112 .

5. Joshua Fairfield and Hannah Shtein, "Big Data, Big Problems: Emerging Issues in the Ethics of Data Science and Journalism," *Journal of Mass Media Ethics* 29, no. 1 (2014): 38–51, https://doi.org/10.1080/08900523.2014.863126.

6. Brandi Grissom, "T-Squared: Why We Unpublished Our Prisoner Database," *Texas Tribune*, July 22, 2013, https://www.texastribune.org/2013/07/22/tdcj-data-errors/.

7. Ibid.

8. Travis Swicegood, "On the Records: Prisoner Database Back Online," *Texas Tribune*, July 30, 2013, https://www.texastribune.org/2013/07/30/prisoner-database-back-online/.

9. Staff, "We're Retiring Our Public-Facing Prison Inmates Database," *Texas Tribune*, June 2020, https://www.texastribune.org/library/data/texas-prisons/.

10. Senthil Kumar B, Aravindan Chandrabose, and Bharathi Raja Chakravarthi, "An Overview of Fairness in Data—Illuminating the Bias in Data Pipeline," in *Proceedings of the First Workshop on Language Technology for Equality, Diversity and Inclusion* (LTEDI 2021, Kyiv: Association for Computational Linguistics, 2021), 34–45, https://aclanthology.org/2021.ltedi-1.5.

11. Julia Angwin and Terry Parris Jr., "Facebook Lets Advertisers Exclude Users by Race," ProPublica, October 28, 2016, https://www.propublica.org/article/facebook-lets-advertisers-exclude-users-by-race.

12. Ibid.

13. Jack Gillum and Ariana Tobin, "Facebook Won't Let Employers, Landlords or Lenders Discriminate in Ads Anymore," ProPublica, March 19, 2019, https://www.propublica.org/article/facebook-ads-discrimination-settlement-housing-employment-credit?token=tCCj2I-FHUtoVSuy7QOrlXw0rpazS0Qn.

14. Jon Keegan, "Facebook Got Rid of Racial Ad Categories. Or Did It?," *The Markup*, July 9, 2021, https://themarkup.org/citizen-browser/2021/07/09/facebook-got-rid-of-racial-ad-categories-or-did-it.

15. Heike Felzmann, Eduard Fosch Villaronga, Christoph Lutz, and Aurelia Tamò-Larrieux, "Transparency You Can Trust: Transparency Requirements for Artificial Intelligence between Legal Norms and Contextual Concerns," *Big Data & Society* 6, no. 1 (2019), https://doi.org/10.1177/2053951719860542.

16. Alexandra S. Levine, "Suicide Hotline Shares Data with For-Profit Spinoff, Raising Ethical Questions," POLITICO, January 28, 2022, https://www.politico.com/news/2022/01/28/suicide-hotline-silicon-valley-privacy-debates

-00002617; John Hendel, "Crisis Text Line Ends Data-Sharing Relationship with For-Profit Spinoff," POLITICO, January 31, 2022, https://www.politico.com/news/2022/01/31/crisis-text-line-ends-data-sharing-00004001.

17. "Data Philosophy," Crisis Text Line, https://www.crisistextline.org/data-philosophy/.

18. Hendel, "Crisis Text Line Ends Data-Sharing Relationship with For-Profit Spinoff."

# 15

# Sports Reporting

Nicole Kraft, The Ohio State University

I spend much of my day, every day, focused on sports. But I own no sports jerseys, cheer for very few teams, and rarely attend games for fun. I am a sportswriter who teaches sports journalism and sports media relations. Amid the instruction on game coverage, interviewing, press conference coverage, profile writing, following the money, and more, we must place a strong academic focus on the ethics and integrity that must be inherent in sports reporting.

Sportswriters of all ages face a fundamental challenge. Most of us get into sports journalism because we are fans, first and foremost. That makes it difficult for so many reasons. How can we separate fan behavior from coverage behavior? How can we report stories that reflect negatively on a team we love? How can we ask tough questions of coaches and players we admire? How can college kids possibly compete with professionals when it comes to covering sports in more prominent conferences? How can we enjoy a game if we are watching it for coverage? The short answer is we do these and more because that is what journalism requires. For sports journalists to do their job, they must work while other people are having fun because, ultimately, serving the public interest must come first.

The ethics of sports coverage are not complicated, but they are relatively hard and fast. Fandom must be checked at the door, no matter how passionate you might be. That is especially challenging when some students pick their college based, in part, on the athletic teams. The most well-repeated and significant rule is no cheering in the press box, which is harder than it might appear. The natural reaction when scoring happens or exciting plays unfold is to, well, cheer. When I take teams of students for their first game coverage, the first instruction I give them when we arrive and the last piece of advice that I tell them before the game starts is not to cheer, and as soon as there is a score or a big play for the home team, what do they do? Yes, someone cheers. The ultimate challenge, says Rob Steen in *Sports Journalism: A Multimedia Primer*, is "balancing objective reporting with local loyalty, the expectations of your readers and editor, and the need to maintain a working relationship with clubs and officials with whom you may have daily contact."[1]

Avoiding the fan space should be obvious, but even professionals sometimes get tangled in the lines that cross between professionalism and fandom. Every semester, I show the video of Ed Littler, sports director at News 5 in Nebraska, who has an extremely uncomfortable exchange seeking an autograph "for a friend" from Iowa football coach Kirk Ferentz.[2] My students squirm just watching it. OK, no autographs, they say. We get it. But try explaining to students that it is inappropriate for the media to partake in a T-shirt giveaway at an NHL game, only to find the off-ice NHL officials carrying the same freebie shirts up to their observation booth. Even better, consider students lucky enough to attend a College Football Bowl game who are "rewarded" with gifts, including vests or jackets, and free backpacks stuffed with enough swag to rival an Oscar party. The professional media not only take these gifts—they actually expect them. Does that mean it's ethical to take something just because it's offered?

An even bigger ethical issue is framing the relationships built within coverage, which includes players, coaches, and the communication professionals who provide our access. There have always been people who wanted to cover sports to get close to players, and that can be an ethical challenge when the people we cover are also the people who live in the same dorm as the reporters, or eat in the same dining halls, or attend the same parties or bars. When does coverage end and life begin?

I was teaching a class with several freshmen student-athletes and my undergraduate teaching assistant was the sports editor of our campus newspaper. One morning, our underage freshmen showed us a photo of them posing with fans—in a campus bar. Whether this was a teachable moment or a news story became a discussion point for the class that day. The fact remains that student-journalists live with, take classes with, and even party with the very athletes they cover and this provides a constant illustration of the tension between being a student and being a journalist.

When it comes to the people who provide us access—sports information directors (SIDs) and communication professionals—the relationship gets even more conflicted. At the collegiate level, access is primarily—sometimes exclusively—provided by the athletics communication staff.

This can mean not only a close relationship but one that has the illusion or reality of restricting negative coverage to ensure continued access. SIDs have somewhat rigid contacts with journalists through formalized and routine media availabilities, and limited interview opportunities with players and coaches, which research says can create bridges as well as barriers.[3] Many reporters have noted that access to players and coaches has decreased with the more formalized nature of "media availability," which limits observational reporting or relationship building through informal conversations, and nearly eliminates exclusive interviews with key sources.

Some other ethics of sportswriting can seem to run counter to the ethics of journalism as a whole. Yes, we get free access to virtually every game we wish to "cover," even though that coverage may involve enjoying the moment as research for a future project. Although it is questionably ethical to use a press pass for a game a writer is not actually covering, that element of research covers a lot of bases.

Free food in the press box is not only OK but expected by reporters. I worked for a team that one playoff series switched out the hot buffet for sandwiches and there was nearly a press box mutiny. The Ohio State press box is renowned for its half-time hot dogs and McDonald's frozen drinks in chocolate, coffee, and fruit flavors, which home and away reporters alike double fist. Other teams provide pregame meals priced well below market value and the Buckeyes offer $12 food vouchers for every reporter covering revenue sports that lack press-box food, such as men's and women's basketball. The main reason cited for free food is the sheer length of time coverage requires, with limited breaks that would be prohibitive to standing in line for concessions or sitting down at a conventional restaurant. The practice makes it possible for some news organizations to cover events that they might not be able to afford otherwise and speeds up the news-gathering process while leading to inside information because of relationships built.[4]

I cover an NHL team for the Associated Press where, before each game, we have dinner in the media dining room, joined by visiting media, communications professionals from both teams, NHL officials, front office staff, and sometimes the general manager. It is not a time for reporting, but it is a time for relationship-building through the proverbial breaking of bread—an opportunity that would be limited without the structure of team-provided food. The fact remains that access is the lifeblood of all sports coverage—much like it exists in coverage of government and politics. Considering how intertwined sports has become with the finances, academics, and societal structure in higher ed and beyond, the need to form meaningful connections has never been more important.[5]

Covering sports at the collegiate level brings with it inherent challenges, but it also provides the unequaled feeling of being part of something bigger than an individual, to bring understanding from within a machine that connects the higher ed space in ways few other elements can. To cover sports is to love sports—or we would find a job with better hours. But with the great power of that job comes the great responsibility to check fandom at the stadium door, and remember we are to observe and report, not to advocate.

We may get free entry to games, but there is an ethical price of admission.

## NOTES

1. Rob Steen (2015) *Sports Journalism: A Multimedia Primer*. 2nd ed. London: Taylor & Francis.

2. Adam Jacobi, "Kirk Ferentz and the Most Awkward Autograph Request You've Ever Seen," SB Nation—Black Heart Gold Pants, August 1, 2011, https://www.blackheartgoldpants.com/2011/8/1/2308702/kirk-ferentz-autograph-awkward-ed-littler-big-ten-media-days.

3. David Welch Suggs, "Tensions in the Press Box: Understanding Relationships Among Sports Media and Source Organizations," *Communication & Sport* 4, no. 3 (2015): 261–81, https://doi.org/10.1177/2167479515577191

4. K. Tim Wulfemeyer, "Ethics in Sports Journalism: Tightening Up the Code," *Journal of Mass Media Ethics* 1, no. 1 (1985): 57–67, https://doi.org/10.1080/08900528509358256.

5. Anderson, "Does the Cheerleading Ever Stop?"

# 16

# Digital Ethics

Julianne H. Newton, University of Oregon

Trying to define digital ethics, much less teach it, is akin to trying to catch a 3-year-old who is already 20 feet ahead of you. Just when you think you're catching up, the rascal pivots, squeals with delight, and runs in another direction to duck behind a bush. As McLuhan and Fiore probed more than half a century ago, "We look at the present through a rearview mirror. We march backwards into the future."[1]

Digital ethics examines the power of communicating in 1s and 0s, in words, images, and sounds—message signals that are transmitted, viewed on screens, heard through speakers or earbuds, and experienced via virtual reality headsets. As we know only too well—and with increasing urgency—that power can be used for good or ill. And even though we know that some of those messages are now created by artificial intelligence, it is essential to remember that this seemingly infinitely complex array of message forms, including AI, originated from the human body/mind, with human digits pressing keys to translate thoughts or instructions into data for immediate transmission—even if the "keys" are ultimately "pressed" by algorithmically initiated bots.

Focusing on our humanness, our shared humanity, made up of more than 8 billion individuals living on this twenty-first-century earth, grounds teaching the ethics of digital media in the personal, a more meaningful and engaging learning experience than focusing students on the endless swirl of our continually evolving digital environment. As Mark Deuze argues, studying media today is best approached ontologically, from "a perspective on life lived in, rather than with, media."[2]

Teaching digital ethics, whether as a standalone course or as a module in an overview course on media or ethics, gives students and instructors alike the opportunity to explore not only the ways we engage digital media but also the impact of digital communication on our ways of feeling, knowing, thinking, expressing, interacting, and living. A combined experiential/reasoned approach can ground students' study of media ethics in remembering that all forms of human communication are experienced through the body's perceptual processes—and that we humans have devised all sorts of ways to extend our bodies through a range of tools, from speech to pencils to telescopes to cameras to computers to algorithms to holograms to robots to satellites to spacecraft.

I begin my course in digital ethics by encouraging students to examine their own views about ethics in general. On the first day of class, I assign them to pairs and ask that they tell each other a story about an "ethics-related moment" from their childhood or teen years and then return to the full class to tell the story they've just heard from a colleague. I tell them an example story from my own life, stress that they do not have to participate if they are not comfortable doing so, and ask the students to agree that their stories stay within the class. The stories usually describe simple events, such as lying about something they did (or didn't do) at school, getting caught taking a toy from a sibling or sneaking into a forbidden place or activity, or deciding whether to tell an adult about something a friend did. Sometimes the stories are intense, revealing significant moments in a young person's life. Invariably, the stories are vivid, because the emotions they felt as young people and the ensuing consequences made them memorable. The discussion that evolves from these storytelling experiences not only introduces students to one another but also reveals that 1) everyone has to learn to behave ethically, and 2) developing a sense of ethics involves a compounded process of thinking, behaving, feeling, making mistakes, and learning to do better.

From there we move into an overview of basic ethical theories, drawing from Stephen Ward's "Ethics in a Nutshell,"[3] which parses ethical approaches into teleological, deontological, and virtue ethics, and noting, as Ward does, that ethical systems can involve aspects of all three approaches. Keeping the theoretical aspects relatively simple gives students without a philosophical background an introductory vocabulary. Students also find Ward's definition of ethics helpful: "Ethics is the dynamic, evolving activity of applying, balancing, and modifying principles in light of new facts, new technology, new social attitudes and changing economic and political conditions."[4] From there, we move quickly into applying the three approaches to discuss concerns in digital ethics, such as:

- data privacy
- mis/disinformation
- deep fakes
- artificial intelligence
- free speech versus responsible speech
- discriminatory practices
- control of communication systems versus regulation
- wearable devices
- access inequities
- digital freedom versus surveillance
- the singularity
- harassment and violence in immersive environments
- the realization that most of us are already cyborgs, given our continual state of connection through smartphones, tablets, watches, and computers

These two strategies—drawing on personal stories and applying basic ethical theory to digital issues—launch the course into a dance between intuition/feelings and reason/thinking, emphasizing that ethics are something we do, as well as believe and think about. In a full course on digital ethics, I facilitate the dance by assigning creative exercises to enhance self-awareness and reading material to build students' knowledge base and abilities to rationally analyze ethical issues. Creative exercises include sending students in small groups to:

1. Art galleries to compare their responses to a work of art,
2. Observe an intersection with one student on each of the four corners to underscore differences in point of view, and
3. Observe an event and compare their different reports of the event.

After completing a creative exercise, which can be done in person or in virtual environments, students report their experiences and share photographs, videos, writings, and sketches via an online discussion board. You may be asking what these creative exercises have to do with digital ethics. They ground the students in their bodily perceptions, increase awareness of individual literal and metaphorical points of view, enhance creative and critical thinking, and facilitate understanding of the challenge and responsibility of communicating truthfully and effectively about something they've experienced, regardless of the medium of communication.

Interspersed between these creative experiences, students write one-page abstracts of key research articles and selections from books about digital ethics. The abstract structure requires students to synthesize a reading in their own words in a short "nugget" paragraph and then apply the core idea of the reading to an image they find online. For example, for an abstract about part I of *Understanding Digital Ethics*,[5] one student posted an image[6] from the Moral Machine experiment,[7] highlighting the surprisingly different moral preferences about autonomous vehicle decision-making expressed by people in different parts of the world. Applying the reading to an image in this way brings the verbal content to life, making the material relevant to everyday topics in students' media repertoires and sparking lively discussions.

An additional experience, assigned in iterative parts throughout the term, requires students to produce a project exploring a digital ethics issue more deeply. The project may be either a research paper examining an issue through scholarly and popular literature or a creative project, such as developing a website or multimedia presentation informing users/viewers about an issue. Projects have ranged from exploring the impact of geotagging on environmental sites to sexual harassment in virtual worlds to why some photographers still prefer film over digital. Students share what they learn in presentations, increasing knowledge for the whole class.

Finally, each student is assigned to develop their own code of ethics with the goal of creating a set of personal ethics that they embrace in their daily life, as well as in professional practice.

For a module of one to two weeks focused on digital ethics within survey ethics or other media courses, I use the personal ethics-related story exercise to enhance self-awareness and readings to facilitate applying the ethics theory discussed earlier in the course to issues in digital ethics. In both survey courses and those focused on digital ethics, I also teach students to play with Marshall and Eric McLuhan's *Laws of Media*[8] via creating a tetrad, exploring the effects of a medium or innovation through four questions:

1. What does _____ enhance?
2. What does it make obsolete?
3. What does it retrieve?
4. When pushed to an extreme, what does it reverse or flip into?[9]

Applying the tetrad to a medium, technology, or idea of their choice advances students' thinking to higher levels of contemplation about the history, development, and potential effects of innovations on culture and society.

As teachers/scholars who study and use media in their many forms, we carry unique responsibilities for teaching our students to understand the power of media, particularly the power of digital media. The numbers, words, images, sounds, and actions we create and send forth into the world extend our minds and hearts toward other people, often with the hope of making the world a better place. Yet we need to consider that what we say and do can help or harm.

My goal in teaching digital ethics through this layered dance of rational and intuitive processing is to give students an opportunity to focus, just for a while, on enhancing their own self-awareness about how they make ethical choices when creating and using digital media. Although such choices rarely fit into a binary ethic of right or wrong, learning to integrate their perceptions, feelings, and rational cognitive processes in a course about their personal role in making decisions as they create and use digital media can help prepare them for a lifetime of continual change and a vast continuum of positive and negative outcomes.

## NOTES

1. Marshall McLuhan and Quentin Fiore, *The Medium is the Massage: An Inventory of Effects* (Bantam Books/Random House, 1967), 75.
2. Mark Deuze, "Media Life," *Media, Culture & Society* 33, no. 1 (2011): 137, https://journals.sagepub.com/doi/10.1177/0163443710386518.
3. Stephen J. A. Ward, "Ethics in a Nutshell: The Nature of Ethics," originally written by Stephen J. A. Ward and modified and expanded by center staff, Center for Journalism Ethics, University of Wisconsin–Madison, https://ethics.journalism.wisc.edu/resources/ethics-in-a-nutshell/.
4. Ward, "Ethics in a Nutshell," paragraph 9.
5. Jonathan Beever, Rudy McDaniel, and Nancy A. Stanlick, *Understanding Digital Ethics: Cases Studies and Contexts* (London: Routledge, 2020).
6. Iyad Rahwan, "File: Moral Machine Screenshot.png," July 1, 2016, Creative Commons Attribution-Share Alike 4.0 International, https://commons.wikimedia.org/w/index.php?curid=98618576.
7. Edmond Awad, Sohan Dsouza, Richard Kim, et al. "The Moral Machine Experiment," *Nature* 563 (2018): 59–64, https://doi.org/10.1038/s41586-018-0637-6.
8. Marshall McLuhan and Eric McLuhan, *Laws of Media: The New Science* (Toronto: University of Toronto, 1988).
9. Andrew McLuhan, "What is A Tetrad?," January 8, 2016, https://medium.com/@andrewmcluhan/what-is-a-tetrad-ad92cb44d4af.

# 17

# Relational Journalism

Paul S. Voakes, Paula Lynn Ellis, and
Lori Bergen, University of Colorado

In the midst of the disruptions and distrust that have plagued traditional news media in recent years, and a degree of polarization rarely seen in American history, a new style of journalism is emerging. Dozens of news organizations, from corporate powerhouses to home-office startups, are reviving a classic role of American journalism: inspiring and enabling Americans to do the difficult, authentic, and ultimately rewarding work of citizenship in a democratic society.

These journalists view their communities not as an audience or customers but as people trying to get common problems solved. They see themselves not as experts controlling the latest information but as participants in a vast ecology of information—and as partners, at times, with community members in the production of news and features. They see their facilitation of community dialog as every bit as important as their actual posting of the story. This kind of journalism is so transparent, so inclusive, and so committed to community-building that it has the potential to bring about a decline in trolling and "fake news" accusations.

We call this approach relational journalism. It recognizes that because no one media outlet alone sets the public agenda, journalism must adapt its role and create unique value. It embraces the full participation of members of the public, all of whom have access to a host of media distribution platforms. Based on our own firsthand observations of this new mindset, these seem to be the key attributes of the practice of relational journalism:

# COMMITMENT TO THE LONG TERM

Most of the commercial journalism in recent decades is characterized by what we call extractive journalism, where the journalist views each source as an opportunity for extraction and then moves on to the next story or project. Now imagine, by contrast, a journalism that is committed to a deeper understanding of citizens' experiences. This will require an open-ended commitment to stay with those involved in an issue or problem for as long as it persists.

## Working with Citizens in Deliberation

Relational journalists help citizens not only to identify ("name") a persistent problem in their community but also to consider options to solving the problem ("frame"). Then begins the difficult job of working through the disagreements and weighing the necessary tradeoffs. Here, too, journalists can contribute—but without becoming advocates for one policy over others. The Solutions Journalism Network, for example, trains journalists to research solutions one community has found for a particular problem in ways that citizens in a different community, with a similar problem, might learn and be inspired. Instead of urging a particular solution, solutions journalists report on what has worked elsewhere. Finally, citizens in deliberation commit to "collective learning" to stay committed and organized for the long term. Journalism again is organized to archive—for easy retrieval—the information from past weeks, months, and years regarding important issues.

## Sharing the Work of Journalism with Citizens

No one group owns or controls the dissemination of new information, as the journalism profession did in the 20th century. That doesn't mean journalism is dying, though—far from it. What it does mean is that journalists must adjust to new ways of working with the citizens formerly known as the audience. In addition to working with citizens on story development, news outlets can easily construct platforms for virtual dialogue, conversation, or debate—dynamics that can facilitate deliberation. They can use the legitimacy of the news organization to guide the conversation toward common values and solutions, and away from language that divides communities.

## New Levels of Diversity and Inclusion

If journalism's facilitative role turns its attention to everyday citizens, and the issues defined by them, it is by necessity increasing the diversity of its work. If by diversity we mean an array of different experiences and different points of view—especially including experiences and points of view and experiences that have historically been overlooked—then relational journalism seems apt for expanding diversity.

Relational journalism presents an intriguing, and likely inspiring, new dimension to the journalism curriculum. It is particularly well-suited to ethics discussions because its theoretical forebear, civic (public) journalism, attracted robust criticism in the 1990s for its perceived ethical breaches. Traditionalists urged adherence to long-standing norms of objectivity, which required detachment and a strict balance between two opposing sides. Public journalists thought that was creating an unnecessary distance between them and community members, and that "bias" on behalf of citizen-centered, democratic practices was entirely acceptable. Traditionalists countered that old-school objectivity was the only sure path to fairness and credibility. How does this debate play out 30 years later?

We've seen appropriate pedagogical homes for relational journalism in both the media and society course and the media ethics course. Here we offer a few pedagogical approaches and discussion prompts that can be applied to either course.

Introducing students to the concept of relational journalism can be a challenge, which is the primary reason we wrote *News for US: Citizen-Centered Journalism*.[1] Articles and essays on relational journalism are appearing with greater frequency, and they're easily searchable. Ours was the first (in the early 2020s) book-length treatment. Fortunately, real-world examples of relational journalism abound, and they're becoming more visible every year.

## JOURNALISM'S ROLE IN A DEMOCRATIC SOCIETY

Once students gain a rudimentary appreciation for the theoretical tenets and essential practices of relational journalism, and an appreciation for its growing popularity among American journalists, they're ready to assess it more critically. One easy entry point, pedagogically, is the media and society course, where students are already addressing high-level abstractions concerning the key institutions and dynamics of a modern democracy. Here we can assess relational journalism in its broadest terms. Our favorite discussion prompts:

- How are citizens represented in the media you consume? Select a recent news report to analyze. What are "ordinary citizens" shown to be doing? How are they portrayed? Is it clear in the story that citizens play a central role in a healthy democracy? If citizens are not represented in the story, how could they be?
- American's trust in news media has steadily declined over the last 80 years. Why do you think so few Americans trust their news media?
- Many traditional journalists have often maintained that the best path to restoring trust in the news media is to double down on the classic dedication to distributing reliable, accurate, objective news reports—and not getting involved with the sources or communities they covered. Do you agree? Why/why not?

## IS RELATIONAL JOURNALISM "ETHICAL"?

In a media ethics course, students are becoming adept at applying moral theories or ethical guidelines as they appraise various journalistic behaviors and decisions. Relational journalism presents a set of values that suggest not only questions of "Will it work?" or "Will it strengthen democratic practice?" but also "Is this an ethical approach to doing journalism?"

Instructors can ask students to investigate the ethics of relational journalism through any number of moral lenses. They may be most familiar with the rule-based, deontological approach suggested by professional codes of ethics, for example: seek the truth; be fair; be accountable; be independent; and monitor society's most powerful institutions, especially for abuse of power. Using a basic knowledge of how relational journalism works, students should be able to assess whether it advances or hinders each of these ethical standards.

Other moral guidelines are a bit more challenging to apply to the doing of journalism—but certainly no less valid. Using the "Golden Mean" of Aristotle or Confucius, students can analyze whether relational journalism provides a sufficient practical balance ("virtue") between extremes. Using Rawls' theory of justice, students can analyze whether relational journalism adequately considers the needs of everyone in a community, especially the least advantaged. Using Mill's principle of utility, students can estimate whether relational journalism is likely to yield consequences that maximize a general good and minimize harm. Using theories of the ethics of care, students can discuss whether relational journalism is sufficiently other-regarding and reciprocal in its dynamics.

Here are two other ethics discussion prompts that require less facility with the moral theories:

- Do you think it is ethical for professional journalists to collaborate with non-journalists? What do you see as the drawbacks? Do the benefits outweigh the drawbacks? Explain.
- Is solutions journalism ethical? Why/why not?

To be sure, relational journalism offers no panacea for what ails American journalism. But we've seen a growing number of journalists who are already committing to deeper listening, to relationships with communities, to honest transparency, to collaborations with citizens that benefit from citizens' wisdom, and to enhancing the community conversations that are already under way. It's an approach that students should be aware of—and be able to assess critically.

## NOTE

1. Paula Lynn Ellis, Paul S. Voakes, and Lori Bergen, *News for US: Citizen-Centered Journalism* (San Diego: Cognella, 2022).

# 18

# Covering Mental Health, Suicide, and Substance Use

Kathleen Bartzen Culver,
University of Wisconsin–Madison

I am an ethicist and a longtime advocate for improved coverage of mental health and suicide in news reporting. I lost a brother to suicide and wrestled many times with how to cover the issue when I worked as a police and courts reporter. I contributed to efforts to transform coverage and reduce stigma. In a recent semester, I was helping student journalists as they worked through how to cover a possible suicide on campus. It was an exceedingly difficult case, and we talked through multiple ethics issues. At one point, one of the editors thanked me for working with them and said, "You know, we've never talked about this in any of my classes."

My heart sank.

Mental health is one of the most important public health issues of our time, and our reporting classes must include attention to it. Decades of research and advocacy have changed for the better the way many in news cover mental health, especially suicide. I advocate for adding these elements of those changes to your reporting courses and evaluation of student work. I also think it's useful for us as educators to offer consultation to student media before and during coverage crises like the one we faced on my campus this year. Suicide is the second leading cause of death for college students,[1] so the issue touches every campus.

## WHAT TO COVER/WHAT NOT TO COVER

Mental health coverage is at its best when framed as the health issue that it is, rather than something that is somehow different from such health issues as nutrition, preventive care, or chronic disease. Solutions-oriented approaches can foster a sense of recovery and hopefulness, rather than emphasizing "struggle." The Solutions Journalism Network[2] offers stories by category, so students can see directly how different outlets have used this approach in the mental health arena.

Major news organizations, including the Associated Press, generally decline to cover any individual suicide unless it is a prominent public figure or the circumstances are publicly disruptive. Experts recommend that stories about suicide not include any discussion of methods used and should never point to a specific event as the "cause" for a person's suicide, such as losing a job. This confuses people by implying that suicide can have one specific cause when the reality is that research shows that a combination of factors leads to people taking their own lives. News outlets must audit their coverage to ensure that attention to mental health is not overly tied to suicide. Suicide is indeed a pressing public health issue, but mental health extends far beyond it.

## LANGUAGE MATTERS

Ethically, reporters would steer entirely clear of the phrasing "committed suicide." The word "committed" implies a criminal act and we, thankfully, are long past the days when the public viewed self-harm as criminal rather than medical. Rather than "committed suicide," use "died by suicide." This extends to suicidal thoughts and actions, as well. Rather than saying a person "considered suicide," use the term "suicidal ideation." Consideration implies a rational calculus while ideation makes it properly clear that no such calculus exists. Reporters should also avoid the phrase "unsuccessful suicide attempt." Instead, state that a person "survived a suicide attempt," remembering that any information like this must be carefully considered and included only when it's absolutely necessary to the story.

## FOCUSING ON RESOURCES

Any coverage involving mental health or suicide is encouraged to include hope-affirming language and links to help. Throughout the country, people can dial 988 from any phone and reach the suicide and crisis support line. The American Foundation for Suicide Prevention recommends the following language near the top and bottom of every story: "If you or someone you know is in crisis, call or text 988 for the Suicide and Crisis Lifeline or contact the Crisis Text Line by texting TALK to 741741." You can help students build muscle memory on this by requiring it as part of all class submissions related to mental health or suicide.

## ACTIVITY IDEAS

You can bring meaningful discussion about reporting on mental health and suicide into your reporting classes in many different ways. Let me offer two thoughts, one simple and one somewhat time intensive. The first is to make use of the Online News Association's Build Your Own Ethics Code tool.[3] Students can sign up for free, log in, and have access to dozens of modules about key journalism ethics concerns, including mental health and suicide. Each module provides background and resources for students to consider. Then they can use a checklist to create their own personal ethics code to guide their reporting now and in the future.

The second idea is to require students take the Johns Hopkins digital course, "Responsible Reporting on Suicide for Journalists."[4] This free, asynchronous online class takes seven hours to complete and is my go-to resource for anyone who wants to learn to do better in this arena. It's entirely research-based, showing how irresponsible reporting can lead to subsequent suicides—known as the contagion effect—while ethical reporting can lead to more people seeking help.

Other organizations have resources you can use:

- AFSP's tips for reporting on suicide[5]
- Reporting on Suicide, an organization dedicated to journalism on these issues[6]
- World Health Organization guidelines[7]
- American Psychiatric Association's suggestions for reporting on mental health[8]

## NOTES

1. American Foundation for Suicide Prevention, *University and College Campus Suicide Prevention*, https://afsp.org/university-and-college-campus-suicide-prevention (accessed June 14, 2023).

2. "What is Solutions Journalism?," Solutions Journalism Network (SJN), https://www.solutionsjournalism.org/.

3. "Build Your Own Ethics Code," ONA Ethics, Online News Association, https://ethics.journalists.org.

4. "Responsible Reporting on Suicide for Journalists," Coursera, https://www.coursera.org/learn/responsible-reporting-on-suicide-for-journalists.

5. "Safe Reporting Guidelines for Media," American Foundation for Suicide Prevention, https://afsp.org/safereporting.

6. "Reporting on Suicide," https://reportingonsuicide.org/.

7. "Preventing Suicide: A Resource for Media Professionals, 2017 Update," World Health Organization/IRIS (Institutional Repository for Information Sharing), https://apps.who.int/iris/handle/10665/258814.

8. "Words Matter: Reporting on Mental Health Conditions," American Psychiatric Association, https://www.psychiatry.org/news-room/reporting-on-mental-health-conditions.

# 19

# Social Media

Sheila B. Lalwani, University of Texas at Austin

A woman decides to run for her country's highest office. The field is crowded, and she begins the election cycle as the front-runner. Not long after, memes emerge of her head on the body of a scantily clad woman with a sexually suggestive message. Another meme circulates with the wording, "Burn the Witch!" The candidate finishes the race dead last. She has several election blunders, but disinformation on social media, particularly Twitter, helps sink her candidacy.

Sound far-fetched? Look no further than the 2021 campaign of Annalena Charlotte Alma Baerbock of Germany, who ran as the only female to replace outgoing long-time Chancellor Angela Merkel, the first woman in German history to hold the office.[1] Baerbock's campaign brought home to the German and European public that misogyny, particularly online, is alive and well.[2] Baerbock ran against other candidates who made similar mistakes, but the tone of online reactions was muted in comparison. The challenge for journalists becomes distinct: How to report on online disinformation? Does it merit public attention? Why? In what way?

Social media refers to the means of interactions among individuals in which they create, share, or exchange information and ideas in virtual communities and networks.[3] David Craig (2021) highlights how social media platforms have magnified and accelerated the ethical challenges that journalists face in their work.[4] Professional journalists must share the journalistic space with those who simply post content on blogs and social media platforms. This leads to a nexus involving social media and ethics that makes for provocative terrain. The work of ethical journalism is frustrated by the intentional manipulation of social media, be it human or automated. The Baerbock case happened in Germany, interestingly the first democratic country to introduce content moderation laws,[5] but the example could easily apply elsewhere. Content moderation laws in Germany proved ineffective at stemming the problem.[6]

Teaching social media in ethics courses is nothing new, and journalism programs have been incorporating such material into ethics courses for decades. From the early days of Classmates, Friendster, MySpace, Orkut, and Facebook, social media has become infused into society and forged a revolution in the teaching of journalistic ethics.[7] An instructor seeking content on social media and ethics would be drowning in material. This is for both good and bad reasons. Social media can be a powerful tool by which to share information. However, it can be, and often is, a vehicle for misinformation and disinformation. Teaching social media ethics courses involves not just looking at the content but also considering the cybersecurity behind social media. Algorithms pose deep ethical quandaries for journalists in their essential role of fostering public discourse on a range of important issues. Considering the role of a journalist in reporting these issues makes for more than just an interesting conversation. The future of the field is partially dependent on the outcome of the conversation.

Stephen Ward minces no words in arguing that social media or digital ethics deals with distinct ethical problems.[8] One of the fundamental challenges he presents is a review of the nature of journalism and the definition of a journalist. He argues that a lack of clarity over these questions contributes to disputes over who is doing journalism.[9] Other important questions relate to the anonymity of social media users, how to handle errors and conflicts of interest, citizen journalists, and the ethics of images.[10] Social media encourages members of the public to share their ideas, but what happens when their sharing becomes toxic?

In the case of Baerbock, individual Twitter users were creating and spreading disinformation. Hashtags like #verdienenwiebaerbock (earnlikebaerbock), #studierenwiebaerbock (studylikebaerbock), #baerbockgate, and #baerplag (short form for plagiarism) trended on Twitter. Many of the memes shared online connected Baerbock to competence and overall likeability—factors that her male counterparts did not experience in the same way. One study found that among women applying for jobs typically occupied by men, youth and attractiveness are detrimental for women.[11] Baerbock was among the youngest females in Germany's history to run for the highest office. Her age and looks were, in some instances, held against her.[12]

The disinformation campaign against Baerbock undermined her credibility. In April 2021, a screenshot that falsely claimed her decision to prevent Germans from keeping pets due to their impact on the climate went viral. Another screenshot claimed that she wanted to abolish the pension for widows. Despite content moderation laws in place and blowback from other Twitter users, the content has been available since it was initially posted. Other candidates in the race faced disinformation, but not nearly to the same extent.[13]

These instances also bring existing ethical debates to bear. For example, since women experience more negative online harassment, what should be the role of the traditional news media in addressing these harms? Women in politics frequently experience the most harmful comments online.[14] The damage from the speed and the power with which they move is hard to reverse. Social media ethics help to revive existing debates, if even with a fresh face. In this way, journalists can contribute to greater awareness of the problem and help protect victims. For students, there are powerful questions to consider on accuracy and bias.

These instances bring up questions of privacy. News organizations in many cases have published their ethics policies. For example, the NPR *Ethics Handbook* puts an emphasis on accuracy.[15] The Associated Press emphasizes respect for journalistic integrity and respect for privacy.[16] Connecting lessons to privacy, disinformation, and misinformation helps journalists understand their professional obligations.

Craig noted that scholars have drawn upon existing ethical frameworks to study social media in the practice of journalism, but gaps in this approach persist.[17] Some scholarship has called for the possibility of universal principles, such as the expanding of common ground on morals and media ethics beyond Western perspectives.[18] Beginning with existing perspectives is a productive start, but given the ubiquitous nature of social media, it should not stop there. The classroom presents an ideal setting to consider these questions.

## NOTES

1. Naďa Kovalčíková and Melanie Weiser, "Targeting Baerbock: Gendered Disinformation in Germany's Election," German Marshall Fund of the United States: Alliance for Securing Democracy, August 30, 2021, https://securingdemocracy.gmfus.org/targeting-baerbock-gendered-disinformation-in-germanys-2021-federal-election/.

2. Ibid.

3. "Social Media Overview," University Communications and Marketing, Tufts University, 2023, https://communications.tufts.edu/marketing-and-branding/social-media-overview/#:~:text=What%20is%20Social%20Media%3F,Instagram%2C%20LinkedIn%20and%20YouTube%20accounts.

4. David A. Craig, "Global Social Media Ethics and the Responsibility of Journalism," Summary, August 31, 2021, Oxford Research Encyclopedias, https://oxfordre.com/communication/display/10.1093/acrefore/9780190228613.001.0001

/acrefore-9780190228613-e-917;jsessionid=92F47964EA1CE41EA3EF0EF5E76C99 E9#acrefore-9780190228613-e-917-div1-1.

5. "Germany Proposes Europe's First Diversity Rules for Social Media Platforms," LSE (blog), May 29, 2019, London School of Economics and Political Science, https://blogs.lse.ac.uk/medialse/2019/05/29/germany-proposes-europes-first-diversity-rules-for-social-media-platforms/.

6. Kristina Wilfore, "The Gendered Disinformation Playbook in Germany is a Warning for Europe," October 21, 2021, Brookings Institution, https://www.brookings.edu/techstream/the-gendered-disinformation-playbook-in-germany-is-a-warning-for-europe/.

7. Stephen J. A. Ward, "Digital Media Ethics," Center for Journalism Ethics, School of Journalism and Mass Communication, University of Wisconsin–Madison, https://ethics.journalism.wisc.edu/resources/digital-media-ethics/.

8. Ibid.
9. Ibid.
10. Ibid.
11. Sebastian Jäckle and Thomas Metz, "Beauty Contest Revisited: The Effects of Perceived Attractiveness, Competence, and Likability on the Electoral Success of German MPs," *Politics & Policy* 45, no. 4 (2017): 495–534, https://doi.org/10.1111/polp.12209.

12. Ibid.
13. Kovalčíková and Weiser, "Targeting Baerbock."
14. Mona Lena Krook, "Violence Against Women in Politics," *Journal of Democracy* 28, no. 1 (January 2017): 74–88, https://www.journalofdemocracy.org/articles/violence-against-women-in-politics/.

15. NPR *Ethics Handbook*, Special Section: Social Media, https://www.npr.org/about-npr/688418842/special-section-social-media.

16. "Social Media Guidelines for AP Reporters," revised May 2013, Associated Press, http://web.archive.org/web/20160616191807/http://www.ap.org/Images/Social-Media-Guidelines_tcm28-9832.pdf.

17. Craig, "Global Social Media Ethics and the Responsibility of Journalism."
18. Ibid.

# 20

# Science, Health, and Environmental Journalism

Rhema Zlaten, Colorado Mesa University

Researchers, journalists, and the public all contribute to culture's understanding of science. The media, in particular, greatly shapes narratives of science for the public. The news media frame scientific research by seeking out relevant public information,[1] and then the public will further reinterpret those frames. Scientists (especially through publicly funded endeavors) are obligated to share information with the public.[2] One of the primary ways this sharing happens is through news media.

When teaching about ethical challenges in science communication, the roles of the researchers, news media, and the public must all be considered. Additionally, training journalists to act as better-educated watchdogs for scientific practices and concerns could result in increased public trust of scientific research. The art of science communication, then, should encompass each of these interconnected sectors. This chapter explores many of the ethical issues that science communicators face in navigating these three groups of people.

## SCIENCE COMMUNICATION TRIANGLE: BIOSAFETY TENSIONS

The laboratory reverse engineering of a super-flu virus strain in 2011 by virologist Ron Fouchier's team unleashed a torrent of discussion about the ethics of biosafety among scientists, news media, and the public. Fouchier's team nudged the H5N1 "bird flu" virus to evolve so it could move between mammals (and not just birds) in an experiment to show how the virus could potentially mutate in the wild to human contagion status.[3] The team rationalized the publishing of their process as a giant leap forward for epidemiology and as a guidebook for how to trace the potential mutation of other superbugs.[4]

To release the recipe, Fouchier's team obtained an export license for weaponized technology from the Dutch government and a review by the US National Institute of Allergy and Infectious Diseases.[5] A 2012 World Health Organization meeting concerning the dissemination of Fouchier's H5N1 mutation recipe also approved the release of the information, primarily as a means to stimulate further research on flu progressions.[6] After the research was published, public debate raged through the news media and research communities concerning the ethicality of "gain-of-function" research, such as Fouchier's H5N1 work.[7] Additionally, many governments imposed stricter oversight on H5N1 research, with the United States even proposing that some H5N1 research be kept secret.[8] Another fallout was that public trust in both science and the press continued to erode as issues of transparency increased surrounding biosecurity research.[9]

Concerns about how experimental virology (such as publishing how to reverse engineer the H5N1 virus) can become tools for harm (such as bioterrorism) contribute to how news media report on scientific advancements of all types. In turn, these media framings can greatly shape how the public will perceive and support the advancements of science.[10] As illustrated by the H5N1 saga, the ethical progression of science is a modern concern at the center of media, public, and scientific consciousness, and news journalists are at the heart of these idea exchanges.

## NEWS FRAMING OF SCIENCE INFORMATION AND PUBLIC TRUST

Researchers and the public maintain a delicate relationship in the quest for furthering science. One Pew Research study found great disparities between the advice given by experts and public opinion on key issues such as biosafety, GMO foods, animal research, and vaccinations. The same study found that 79 percent of American adults are confident in the benefits to people provided by science as a field.[11] There seems to be a widening distrust of scientists but a continued reverence of science as an American ideology. What causes this disparity?

Several studies point to news media framing of scientific issues as contributing to the erosion of public trust in science.[12] Richard Holliman described news media as the prominent informants of science to the public.[13] Scientists seem to engage in a love/hate relationship with the pervasive power of media to both build and destroy their fields of inquiry.

Another Pew Research study on science and communication found that 43 percent of scientists value promotion of their work in news media.[14] Conversely, 79 percent of scientists are concerned about news reports not distinguishing between "well-founded and not well-founded scientific findings," and 52 percent of scientists also saw that the "simplification of scientific findings is a major problem for science in general."[15] As scientists promote acceptance of their research results, they must also balance the tension of how to best express their area of expertise to the media and how to relay the information in the best format possible for broad public understanding.

One way journalists convert scientific knowledge to public knowledge is through the use of metaphor, usually in a quest to explain complex scientific terms, such as media coverage of the "Frankenfood" campaign launched by Greenpeace in 1992. The framing of genetically modified food as the "monstrous work of science gods" resonated in the public for the decades following the release of the Greenpeace campaign even though the rhetoric originated from the minds of anti-GMO groups.[16] This equation of Frankenstein creations to science continues today, especially in issues of biosafety, such as synthetic biology.[17]

Media workers reporting on scientific issues and developments must consider the power of their metaphorical pen. When the press attaches words like "threat" or "danger" to scientific research, the editorial team releasing the story must consider deeply if that threat is truly present and the level of such dangers. The far-reaching effects of media campaigns (such as the Frankenfood campaign) led some people to argue that news media sensationalize science. In their role as watchdog, the press must cover issues concerning public safety. The unfortunate aftereffect of such coverage is often the stigmatization of that particular idea or field, leading to disparity in the public and scientific viewpoints. A primary objective of journalists writing about science, then, is to communicate with delicacy and reason in order to avoid sensationalized phrasing.

## ASSIGNMENT INSPIRATIONS FOR TEACHING SCIENCE COMMUNICATION ETHICS

The scientific community is ethically obligated to keep the public safe and inform the public about evolving research, especially when issues with global implications are at stake. The press, in turn, has an ethical obligation to correctly frame science for the public in addition to acting as a watchdog for scientific discourse. Additionally, the public must demand (and participate in) such conversations when they arise. An ethical news framework that balances scientific community needs with public needs begins with an understanding of basic scientific research terms such as correlation, causality, and statistical validity. When journalists first ask questions of researchers around the creation and safety measures of their study design, this creates a strong and well-founded discussion about impact for the audience. In this way, news media can play a big role in helping scientific debates gain public discourse and decision-making power, which can lead to stricter guidelines for funding risky research, such as what played out for H5N1 research in the 2010s.[18] The following assignment ideas will lead your students in discussions about transparency, responsibility, background research, and sensationalism in science communication.

### ASSIGNMENT IDEA 1

*"Rare meteor dust cures cancer!"*
*Crafting a news story based on recent scientific findings*

- In class, provide students with a recently published scientific study. Also include quotes from interviews with the scientists (you could either craft your own quotes and tell them they are fictitious or see if there are any press releases available on the study). Tell the students they will either be writing a news story based on the study, or that they will craft an outline to a news story, depending on the type of reporting and/or science communication class you are teaching, and also the level of the students.
    a. Before the students begin their story, ask them to answer these questions:
        - How was this study conducted? (Consider sample size; replication; validity; etc.)
        - How does this particular study fit in with other studies of similar topic?
        - Why is this particular study novel? Or what does this study contribute to human understanding of the world?
        - Who funded the research of this study?
        - What claims of relevance have the scientists made about this study? How might you fact-check those claims? Did the scientists inflate their results?
        - Have either you (or the scientist) conflated causation and correlation when thinking about the results of the study?
        - Are there potential environmental, global, health, or safety concerns about this research? What are they and why?
        - What is the main key finding of this study that is relevant to the public?

- After their brainstorm document is complete, instruct students to write a 500- to 750-word news story covering the scientific article including background info, the major claim of relevance to the public, potential implications to readers of the research, and any potential concerns.

### ASSIGNMENT IDEA 2

*Framing of science in the media*

- Before class, provide students with a recently published scientific study and then also a news media piece about that same study. For the scientific study, highlight relevant sections to read.
- In class, assign students to groups of 3–4. Ask each group to compare the two articles. What is different? What is similar? How did the writer of the news article describe the findings of the scientific study? What types of metaphors did the journalist use to describe the study?
- After small-group discussion time, bring the entire class back together to share their findings and then ask the entire class these questions: What was confusing about either of the articles? Was there any missing information? Do you think the news article was a fair representation of the scientific study? Why or why not? Do you think the public will trust the science findings based on the news article that was written?
- If you have time to take the assignment one step further, have the groups reconvene and research public responses to the scientific news article on social media platforms. Assign each group a different social media platform to search for responses, and then compare how the public responded to the article across these different platforms. One group could also research if the scientists of the original study responded to the news article.

### NOTES

1. Jay Hmielowski, Lauren Feldman, Teresa A. Myers, Anthony Leiserowitz, and Edward Maibach, "An Attack on Science? Media Use, Trust in Scientists, and Perceptions of Global Warming," *Public Understanding of Science* 23, no. 7 (2013): 866.

2. Kristofer Hansson, Susanne Lundin, Jekaterina Kaleja, and Aivita Putnina, "Framing the Public: The Policy Process around Xenotransplantation in Latvia and Sweden 1970–2004," *Science and Public Policy* 38, no. 8 (2011): 629.

3. David Malakoff, "H5N1 Researchers Announce End of Research Moratorium," *Science*, January 23, 2013, http://www.sciencemag.org/news/2013/01/h5n1-researchers-announce-end-of-research-moratorium.

4. Nell Greenfieldboyce, "Scientists Publish Recipe for Making Bird Flu More Contagious," *Shots: Health News from NPR*, National Public Radio, April 10, 2104, http://www.npr.org/blogs/health/2014/04/10/301432633/scientists-publish-recipe-for-making-bird-flu-more-contagious.

5. Ibid.

6. Celeste M. Condit, "Insufficient Fear of the 'Super-flu'?: The World Health Organization's Global Decision-Making for Health," *Poroi: An Interdisciplinary Journal of Rhetorical Analysis and Invention* 10, no. 1 (2014): 3.

7. Malakoff, "H5N1 Researchers Announce End of Research Moratorium."

8. David Malakoff, "Proposed H5N1 Research Reviews Raise Concerns," *Science* 338, 6112 (2012): 1271, https://www.science.org/doi/10.1126/science.338.6112.1271.

9. Cary Funk and Lee Rainie, "Public and Scientists' Views on Science and Society," Pew Research Center, January 29, 2015, http://www.pewinternet.org/2015/01/29/public-and-scientists-views-on-science-and-society/.

10. Brigitte Gschmeidler and Alexandria Seiringer, "'Knight in Shining Armour' or 'Frankenstein's Creation'? The Coverage of Synthetic Biology in German-Language Media," *Public Understanding of Science* 21, no. 2 (2012): 164, https://doi.org/10.1177/0963662511403876.

11. Funk and Rainie, "Public and Scientists' Views on Science and Society."

12. Hmielowski et al., "An Attack on Science?"

13. Richard Holliman, "Media Coverage of Cloning: A Study of Media Content, Production and Reception," *Public Understanding of Science* 13, no. 2 (2004): 108–9.

14. Lee Rainie, Cary Funk, and Monica Anderson, "How Scientists Engage the Public," Pew Research Center, February 15, 2015, http://www.pewinternet.org/2015/02/15/how-scientists-engage-public/.

15. Raine, Funk, and Anderson, "How Scientists Engage the Public."

16. Jennifer Welchman, "Frankenfood, or Fear and Loathing at the Grocery Store," *Journal of Philosophical Research* 32, supplement (2007): 141.

17. Gschmeidler, and Seiringer, "Knight in Shining Armour," 169.

18. Brendan Maher, "New Guidelines Announced for Risky Research," (news blog), *Nature*, February 21, 2013, https://blogs.nature.com/news/2013/02/new-guidelines-announced-for-risky-research.html.

# 21

# Foreign Correspondence

Sheila B. Lalwani, University of Texas at Austin

The ethical considerations foreign correspondents must undertake are not unlike that of other, domestic journalists, but the stakes are higher. I believe that this factor alone makes a case for revamping ethics education at the graduate level to include this component. Reporting from overseas, which I did for various assignments, exposes the wider public to a form of cultural interpretation that they may not otherwise experience.[1] This specific type of reporting affirms the role of journalists as agenda-setters and opinion leaders who influence the public and help to shape foreign policy.[2] This is not a small responsibility.

Graduate programs can use foreign reporting as a prism to revamp aspects of an ethics curriculum. I have taught international journalism for years primarily to undergraduate and MA-level students and make it a point to incorporate into the class. I developed two courses on international journalism, one for a semester-length class at the University of Leipzig, and another for the Philip Merrill College of Journalism at the University of Maryland. I was able to report from overseas at several junctures during my career as a journalist. I write this chapter from the viewpoint of a former reporter who wants to see a pipeline of talented journalists enter the field, and, hopefully, make it better.

I have come across many graduate students aspiring to report from overseas. Despite shuttering foreign bureaus, shaky interest in foreign news among domestic audiences, and dwindling full-time foreign correspondent positions, an appetite for international news remains in place—and so does the need to report with integrity. Let's explore the traditional values of foreign correspondence as essential fixtures in the practice of journalism and the major challenges facing foreign correspondents.

## FOREIGN REPORTING AND ETHICS

Like much of journalism, foreign correspondence has experienced turbulent changes. Despite the proliferation of cable, satellite television, internet, radio, and social media platforms, interest in international news is limited.[3] Delivering news from overseas is expensive and media ownership has become much more concentrated, placing an emphasis on profits.[4] With the *New York Times* and *Washington Post* as notable exceptions, news organizations have shuttered foreign bureaus, laid off foreign correspondents, or cut back on foreign news altogether.[5] Of the many ways of interpreting this set of facts, at least one of them is the affirmation that foreign reporting must be truthful, accurate, and fair. The role of foreign correspondents as agenda-setters, news producers, and opinion leaders with an important mission to fulfill becomes more evident.

The first challenge ethics professors must confront is to situate foreign reporting within their courses, while formally studying the moral beliefs and principles behind cutting back on this subset of journalism. Øyvind Kvalnes created the Navigation Wheel as a tool for when journalists face ethical dilemmas in social media use, but it may also help students navigate through the thorny issues underlying foreign correspondence.[6] The Navigation Wheel also guides decision-makers in considering questions related to identity, morality, law, ethics, reputation, and economics. Kvalnes points out that the priority of questions relies on the context and is up to the decision-maker. A suggestion is to run through the relevant options achievable and consider the arguments as a foundation for coming to a conclusion.[7]

This approach may represent a break from traditional ethics training. Ethics courses have often focused on key domestic cases, philosophers, and principles, such as Immanuel Kant's categorical imperative, reporter-source privilege, etc. To create a module on foreign reporting within an ethics course, it may be useful to connect the traditional values of journalism—trust, truth, independence, fairness, accuracy, and humanity—as the building blocks that helped to shape foreign reporting. To do this, I have highlighted the towering figures of foreign correspondents who reported during the "Golden Age," that is, 1930–1945.[8] Ernie Pyle, the great World War II foreign correspondent, often comes up. Pyle was known for connecting World War II to the human face of suffering. Troops trusted and confided in him. Pyle won a Pulitzer Prize[9] for this work, but the story speaks to the power of honest and accurate reporting and its ability to transcend generations.

## PARACHUTE JOURNALISM AND PARTIAL TRUTHS

A challenge ethics professors must consider concerns one of the primary challenges of foreign reporting: parachute journalism. This refers to journalists descending upon a particular area for a specific reason and limited time.[10] Economic constraints have made editors reluctant to dispatch reporters to other parts of the world unless there is a major story unfolding, such as war, natural disasters, or humanitarian crises. This is what Susan Moeller refers to as the "Four Horsemen of the Apocalypse" syndrome: conflict, death or assassination, famine, and pestilence.[11] A relentless, albeit temporary, focus tends to warp reality.[12]

One illustrative example concerns Ethiopia, which during the 1980s was struck by one of the worst famines the world had ever seen.[13] Images of emaciated children and women in the desert became seared in the minds of millions. Years after the famine had passed, memories of those images lingered. Another example is Turkey, where a 2023 earthquake left thousands dead. Media descended on Istanbul. Once the rebuilding began, the media left. When I have discussed this with students, they agree that foreign correspondence can do better. In-class exercises that prod students to come up with a running list of stories are valuable. What can they report on once they have left? What footage should they capture? How can they go back? Are there anniversaries or other milestones they can work into the news? How can they incorporate people? I brought up these points during one class, and students struggled to identify reporting strategies to prevent parachute journalism until I suggested ideas like anniversaries, human interest pieces, the impact of an event or policy on different groups, and visual storytelling techniques as means to continue reporting on an issue. The major takeaway from that exercise was that students, who may have previously heard that keeping numbers, names, and a running list of story ideas are important for journalists, began to understand why. The major learning: good ideas beget more good ideas.

## SYSTEMIC BIAS IN FOREIGN REPORTING

Foreign reporting is often stereotypic and rooted in opinions, prescriptions, and superficial understanding. This becomes problematic when considering that foreign reporting fuels the public's understanding of the outside world. Numerous countries and continents have experienced this problem, but perhaps none more so than the Global South. Ngugi pointed out that the impression of Africa among American audiences is considerably dependent on the coverage they experience through the media.[14] In the framing of Africa, coverage is often racist and stereotypic.[15]

Latin America and Asia have experienced similar biases in coverage. Hafner-Burton and Ron analyzed the coverage of Latin America among three leading Anglo-American media sources from 1981 to 2000 and found that news disproportionately portrayed abuses there in terms of human rights as compared to other world regions.[16] Their study concluded that the region's proximity to the United States and its relevance to US policy debates fueled this bias.[17] In Asia, most of the coverage focuses on India and China, with other countries receiving limited coverage. For example, when Timor-Leste struggled with its elections, coverage focused on that rather than on the important gains it had achieved since becoming an independent nation.

Systemic bias also extends to individuals, groups of people, and faith systems, such as women, members of the LGBTQIA+ communities, and faith groups. Despite women being at near parity for reporting positions in newsrooms, international coverage remains uneven. The "Year of the Woman" was 2018, but women were curiously absent from news coverage.[18] This bias has carried over into foreign reporting as well. For example, women are often portrayed as victims. Giotis has called for a shift in how foreign correspondents portray women, calling on coverage to be less depictive of them as victims and to highlight their agency.[19]

## NOTES

1. Pierre Bourdieu, *The Field of Cultural Production: Essays on Art and Literature*, edited and introduced by Randal Johnson (New York: Columbia University Press, 1993).

2. Philip M. Seib, *Headline Diplomacy: How News Coverage Affects Foreign Policy* (Westport, CT: Praeger, 1997).

3. John Maxwell Hamilton and Eric Jenner, "Redefining Foreign Correspondence," Joan Shorenstein Center on the Press, Politics and Public Policy, Working Paper Series, Harvard University, 2002, https://shorensteincenter.org/wp-content/uploads/2012/03/2003_02_hamilton_jenner.pdf.

4. Ibid.

5. Ibid.

6. Øyvind Kvalnes, *Digital Dilemmas: Exploring Social Media Ethics in Organizations* (Cham: Palgrave McMillan, 2020), https://link.springer.com/book/10.1007/978-3-030-45927-7.

7. Ibid., 55–56.

8. American Foreign and War Correspondents, *Holocaust Encyclopedia*, United States Holocaust Memorial Museum, https://encyclopedia.ushmm.org/content/en/article/american-foreign-and-war-correspondents.

9. "Ernie Pyle: The Voice of the American Soldier in World War II," Profile, April 17, 2020, National WWII Museum, https://www.nationalww2museum.org/war/articles/ernie-pyle-world-war-ii.

10. Isabel Macdonald, "'Parachute Journalism' in Haiti: Media Sourcing in the 2003–2004 Political Crisis," *Canadian Journal of Communication* 33, no. 2 (2008): 213–32, http://ezproxy.lib.utexas.edu/login?url=https://www.proquest.com/scholarly-journals/parachute-journalism-haiti-media-sourcing-2003/docview/219576106/se-2.

11. Susan D. Moeller, *Compassion Fatigue: How the Media Sell Disease, Famine, War, and Death* (New York: Routledge, 1999).

12. Ibid., 14.

13. John Sorenson, "Mass Media and Discourse on Famine in the Horn of Africa," *Discourse & Society* 2, no. 2 (1991): 223–42, http://www.jstor.org/stable/42888736

14. Muiru Ngugi, "Foreign Correspondents and the Imagination of Africa," in *Media in the Global Context*, edited by Emmanuel K. Ngwainmbi (Cham: Palgrave McMillan, 2019), 229–43. https://link.springer.com/chapter/10.1007/978-3-030-26450-5_10. See also, Susan Goldberg, "For Decades, Our Coverage was Racist. To Rise Above Our Past, We Must Acknowledge It," *National Geographic*, March 12, 2018, https://www.nationalgeographic.com/magazine/article/from-the-editor-race-racism-history.

15. Tom Murphy, "Foreign Correspondents in Africa Still Struggle to Tell the Whole Story," (blog), *Christian Science Monitor*, March 14, 2013, https://www.csmonitor.com/World/Africa/Africa-Monitor/2013/0314/Foreign-correspondents-in-Africa-still-struggle-to-tell-the-whole-story.

16. Emilie Hafner-Burton and James Ron, "The Latin Bias: Regions, the Anglo-American Media, and Human Rights," *International Studies Quarterly* 57 (2013): 474–91, https://ehb.ucsd.edu/pdfs/latin_bias.pdf.

17. Ibid., 486.

18. Gabby Deutch, "In the 'Year of the Woman,' Many Were Missing from International Reporting," *Atlantic*, February 11, 2019, https://www.theatlantic.com/international/archive/2019/02/gender-bias-persists-international-reporting-atlantic/582235/.

19. Chrisanthi Giotis, "More Than a Victim: Thinking Through Foreign Correspondents' Representations of Women in Conflict," in *Rethinking Transitional Gender Justice*, edited by Rita Shackel and Lucy Fiske (Cham: Palgrave McMillan, 2019), https://link.springer.com/chapter/10.1007/978-3-319-77890-7_6.

# IV

# ETHICS BEYOND THE CLASSROOM

# 22

# Teaching the Ethics of Civic Journalism

Mark Poepsel,
Southern Illinois University–Edwardsville

Teaching students to practice civic journalism ethically means preparing them to have their personal sense of journalism ethics and their core sense of social ethics challenged more or less constantly when engaging with audiences. Networked communication spaces leave them perpetually exposed to criticism and bad faith actors while also connecting them to potential wellsprings of support and assistance that can make real community impacts through journalism. To prepare students to navigate the ethics of contemporary civic journalism, it will take everything we know about journalism ethics and then some.

A quick definition of civic journalism is that it is an approach to the practice in which audiences are invited to participate in setting news agendas and in covering the news. The level of community participation differs from organization to organization, project to project. When professional journalists share their limited but powerful authority to shape public opinion with community members, people in the community may form new connections with the news and with each other. They may feel recognized, represented, and empowered. On the other hand, when journalists fail to think critically about how social media content and their own engagement projects might be hijacked and turned into vehicles for misinformation and disinformation, they end up doing more harm than good.

This discussion covers some of the ethical challenges recognized in early civic/public journalism efforts and then quickly moves to address some of the challenges current students are likely to face when practicing civic journalism in a media environment dominated by social networks, search engines, and artificial intelligence (AI). Tips for teaching, including general strategies, discussion questions, and ideas for exercises, are included in each section.

## FIRST: DO NO PR

Civic journalism efforts started as a way for news organizations to reconnect with newspaper audiences who were steadily turning to other news and information sources in the 1980s and 1990s. Some in the news industry felt that newspapers were losing touch with their communities, as local papers were being swallowed up by larger chains and later by even larger media conglomerates. Civic journalism had many sincere adherents, but in some news organizations, it was a shallow public relations effort. The first key ethical lesson of the civic journalism movement is that audiences will recognize, and will likely reject, efforts that only pay lip service to community involvement. PR done in the name of civic journalism engagement to try to recruit readers and subscribers can erode trust in the organization and alienate audiences.

### Tips for Teaching

Your strategic goal should be to introduce students to civic journalism without unintentionally encouraging them to do public relations for a news brand. Consider incorporating these discussion questions with each civic/engagement journalism assignment:

- Have we identified all the key stakeholders and made multiple, sincere efforts to collaborate?
- What are the likely outcomes of this civic journalism project?
- Do they benefit stakeholders as much as the news organization?

Consider assigning students embarking on a civic journalism project of any size to develop a "Reality Checklist" where they list the major stakeholders for a project, what it will take to garner meaningful participation with them, and whether the likely outcomes of a project will benefit each stakeholder group at least as much as the news organization.

## SECOND: NO HALF MEASURES

Even well-meaning and relatively well-resourced civic journalism efforts in the past often left audiences no better off than they had been before the effort to engage. This raised deep ethical concerns in the public that were not fully addressed by the news industry during the initial rise of the civic journalism movement. News organizations were careful during the first wave of the movement in the 1990s and early 2000s to think about what could go wrong if certain members of the public or groups had too much influence over journalists' reporting.

This brought to the public's attention a double standard. They could see powerful individuals and institutions influencing the way news stories were covered and sometimes whether topics were covered at all. At the same time, journalists involved in civic reporting projects often went out of their way to make clear that they would not be unduly swayed by citizens' concerns and opinions. In this way, some of these projects reinforced social hierarchies having a net negative effect on public trust.

Community members do not necessarily differentiate between publisher and journalist. It does not matter to community members if civic reporting projects are limited in ways that are beyond journalists' control. Historically, it was not unusual for journalists working on these projects to set out to find problems in government or problems with "partisanship" that they might address only to find that members of the public did not hold the same goals for public discourse and policy change that journalists thought they should. With some civic journalism efforts, it appeared to the public that journalists were seeking the wrong outcomes. Even if they had the right goals in mind, they had no means of bringing about real change. Journalists who set out to be helpful in their community sometimes came face-to-face with harsh realities about the limits of the profession.

Historically and in current civic/engagement journalism efforts, Black, Indigenous, People of Color (BIPOC) communities, and people of relatively low socioeconomic status are attuned to the failures of mainstream journalism to effect change. People do not trust that news organizations that are part of powerful media corporations have an interest in making systemic change. A half-hearted civic journalism project is not going to convince audiences otherwise.

## Tips for Teaching

Your strategic goal should be to instill in students that half-hearted civic/engagement journalism efforts could do more harm than good in terms of establishing trust with communities. Consider incorporating these discussion questions with each civic/engagement journalism assignment:

- Can we list the potential positive and negative outcomes of this project for all of the key stakeholder groups?

- Do we have the resources and fortitude to see the project through until most or all of the positive outcomes are reached?
- Are any stakeholder groups more likely to benefit from our project in the short run as opposed to the long term? What is the risk, if any, that we might bring about improvements for one group at a cost to other groups?

Consider assigning students a "Reduce, Recycle, Refuse" challenge where they analyze a proposed engagement journalism project to see if the scope needs to be scaled down, if the project needs to be put on the shelf until more favorable conditions are in place, or if an idea should simply be scrapped.

## THIRD: YOUR BACKLASH IS SHOWING

Civic/engagement journalism ethics might simply be characterized as regular journalism ethics practiced transparently in front of community members. When communities rejected some projects in the 1990s and 2000s, they were often rejecting the professional practice or malpractice of ethics. Citizens would, at times, take their concerns about all of the mainstream media into meetings with local journalists who had little to no authority over how national news was produced. Citizens, at times, wanted to discuss journalism ethics on the grand scale while journalists wanted to focus on a specific project with set parameters meant to address a timely issue in their city or local community.

Community members were sometimes accused of having the "wrong agenda." As the public rejected aspects of the civic journalism movement, a backlash in the industry arose. Some news outlets blamed their audiences for project failures. This did not improve public trust, to the extent that members of the public were aware of the industry backlash. In hindsight, it became clear to many that few news organizations were mature enough ethically to actually do civic journalism with positive social outcomes in mind.

### Tips for Teaching

Your strategic goal should be to avoid backlash among your students and in your student media organizations that might arise from a failed or ineffectual engagement project. Consider focusing internally first and have your class or student media organization work through the Dimensions of Difference Guide.[1] The purpose of this guide is to think deeply about the identities of each journalist, about the shared values and ideals of the news organization, and to see where those match and where they might not match with communities. Use the discussion topics and exercises in this guide to suit the scope of your course or project.

## FOURTH: DÉJÀ VU ALL OVER AGAIN

Some key questions that arose in the 1990s and 2000s can be reframed for today's engagement journalism movement to offer guidance to students. One of the primary questions journalists working on civic journalism projects reiterated was: "In civic journalism, how much should the public influence what we cover and how we cover it?" The underlying assumption was that journalists could be objective and that commercially well-connected news organizations could work in the public interest for structural improvement. Historically, though, professional news organizations, at least in the United States, consolidated around advertising revenues and an economically liberal point of view. Thus, the question about public influence was not if the public might lead journalists away from the pristine norm of objectivity but if civic journalism might challenge the pro-business foundation of news organizations, which kept journalists on different lengths of leash.

In contemporary times, journalists have to consider not only the economic position of their news organization but the broader push to market themselves globally as individual brands. If anything, economic forces today are global, regional, and personal. Thus, a better question in a networked environment for civic journalism practice might be, "How far should journalists be willing to go to build and maintain audiences in networked spaces?" Journalism educators must be transparent about the economic realities facing professionals today to prepare students to engage ethically.

Contemporary civic journalism efforts are often developed in partnership with social media platforms. It may not be ethical in general to submit thoughtful, fact-checked journalism to the morass of stream-of-consciousness social media flows. Social media organizations serve content to audiences using algorithms meant to increase engagement and length of time spent on the platform with little regard for the quality of content. Because news needs audiences, and social media dominate networked communication spaces, we do what we must, but we do have control over which platforms we work with and how we work with them. We must craft and continuously refine ethical guidelines for engaging with audiences in these spaces.

Sometimes journalists incorporate information found on social media platforms as a kind of "civic journalism-lite." Students must be prepared to critically analyze where social media posts originate. Verification on Twitter (X), as of 2023, can be bought. On many platforms, basic measures of reach can be manipulated by bots and by groups of human users more interested in creating chaos than informing people. If information from human sources needs to be double-checked, social media information needs to be triple-checked for accuracy, origin, and relevance.

**Tips for Teaching**

Your strategic goal should be to prepare students to engage with audiences on social media platforms in ways that enhance students' professional standing without leading them into one of the many ethical pitfalls that riddle the social media landscape. You may incorporate these discussion questions with each civic/engagement journalism assignment:

- How do students plan to present themselves on social media?
- Which platforms are best for professional engagement and why?
- What changes can we anticipate in the coming months and years for different popular social media platforms?
- What ethical norms should be standard practice across all social media platforms for early career professional journalists?

One option is assigning students the "Build a Raft of Support" assignment. In this exercise, students identify their personal brand based on the types of journalism in which they hope to practice most often. Students then consider 3–5 social media platforms where they might present themselves professionally. Students should list what considerations they plan to employ each and every time they post to these platforms. Additionally, students should identify and list which platforms they are willing to cite in their reporting. They should then list what considerations they plan to employ for verification purposes each and every time they quote another user on one of these platforms.

## FIFTH: A PLEA

Another key ethical question journalists raised in early civic journalism projects had to do with how the practice was being influenced on the large scale. Journalists would ask questions like this: "If I practice civic journalism, does that mean I have to let the public tell me how to do my job?" This spoke to concerns not just about individual news stories or news projects but about journalistic routines and organizational and industry norms and values. On one hand, connecting with communities and sharing in the agenda-setting function of the news media could be a boon to the industry, a way to reconnect with audiences and to reach out, not just person-to-person but institution-to-institution, as leaders in key civic organizations were sometimes invited in for listening sessions or other collaborations in civic journalism exercises. The downside, some feared, was that news outlets would trend even more toward pandering to audience fears, pop culture interests, and personal interest news. Covering city hall and school board meetings was not always atop citizens' agendas, but journalists argued it was their ethical and professional duty to act as a watchdog.

The danger in contemporary engagement journalism is that journalists will strive to be both popular social media news and thought influencers and that they will still be expected to follow more traditional news routines as well. This would stretch already-tapped news staffs even more thinly. Journalists' work-life balance is a matter of journalism ethics. An industry that burns through professionals is not likely to bring its practitioners to ethical maturity. If contemporary journalists are going to practice engagement journalism as a matter of routine, the resources to support them must be adequate. If the most full-fledged version of civic/engaged journalism practice is the maintenance of thoughtful networked spaces where communities seek to recognize what works and what does not work for them—amidst massive flows of vitriol, misinformation, and disinformation—it is not ethical to send journalists into the fray of networked communication battle without proper support.

**Tips for Teaching**

Your strategic goal should be to prepare students to advocate for professional support with the same sense that you would not send soldiers to battle without weapons or tools of evasion and defense. Incorporate these discussion questions into your course and ask them multiple times to gauge how students' attitudes and preparations evolve:

- What are your expectations, pros and cons, for engaging with audiences when you practice engagement journalism?
- What types of outcomes do you hope to achieve through your journalism work?
- How do you expect the industry to evolve in terms of engagement journalism throughout your career?
- What are your career goals in terms of developing a "personal brand" in journalism?
- What types of professional support do you expect from news organizations throughout your career?

- What are some, more or less, universal ethical principles that all journalists working online and engaging with audiences should adopt and adhere to?

You may assign students a final essay in this course in which they address the following topics in one or two paragraphs each: 1) Whether engagement journalism is more likely to be a routine practice for most journalists, or a special set of projects done in select news organizations; 2) What exciting engagement journalism stories, projects, or routines would "make it all worthwhile" considering the challenges addressed throughout this chapter; 3) What ethical concerns that have not been raised in this chapter might they anticipate in light of ongoing changes to social media platforms?

## CONCLUSION

Today's local journalism conflicts hit differently than those of the 1990s and early 2000s. Some of the extreme rhetoric of that age is reaching policy stages at the local level, on a national scale.

- City council meetings are about racial and economic disparities in housing and business opportunities.
- School board meetings are about beating back the swells of global fascism.
- State and local elections are about whether girls might have to bear their rapist's or their father's baby.

When and if we set up open spaces for public debate to be moderated by professional journalists, we need to ask if they are prepared for the threats they might face and for the psychological trauma of facing people who consider them not just a nuisance but an enemy.

Civic/engagement journalism projects are often done in news organizations' proprietary spaces. This demands certain levels of control and responsibility. All engagements with the public should be recorded and saved in case of instances of malicious editing. Academics call it "dark participation," the manipulation of social media content and audience-journalist interactions to promote extreme agendas.[2] We can ethically protect the field if we practice diligence in managing discussions in proprietary online spaces. Thus, we can ethically protect news content, news practices, and news organizations in an industry where engagement and hostility are both increasing. At least, we can try.

## NOTES

1. "Dimensions of Difference Newsroom Guide," Trusting News: A Project of RJI and API, Reynolds Journalism Institute and American Press Institute, http://trustingnews.org/dimensions.

2. Thorsten Quandt, "Dark Participation," *Media and Communication* 6, no. 4 (2018), https://www.cogitatiopress.com/mediaandcommunication/article/view/1519.

# 23

# Media Ethics is for Everyone
Joseph Jones, West Virginia University

The words "communication" and "community" share the same root in Latin, meaning to make common or to share. Community is created by talking things out and communicating with one another to build a world in common and share specific meanings. Our very society is thus made *via* communication. There is not something called society that pre-exists and then expresses itself through communication. It is through the very act of communicating that society comes into existence.[1] As people are socialized into specific cultures, communication is also a central aspect of constituting individuals. Our identities and choices on how we build, understand, and negotiate the world depend upon how we articulate, circulate, and exchange particular forms of meaning. It is thus through communication that our humanity—our very selves—comes into being.[2] By way of culturally specific messages, we continually *become* who we are. This is what makes media ethics education so central. Not only are we asking how we can make ethical media creators, we also consider the social role of media and how we can create quality messages that invite people to become the best versions of themselves.

When preparing for (and adapting to) the future of media ethics, it is crucial to understand the ontological, epistemological, and axiological relationship between media, self, and society. Knowing how these seemingly separate entities co-constitute one another in historically specific contexts enables a more comprehensive view of relevant ethical issues and the processes by which new issues arise and are addressed—or ignored. If the media are largely responsible for inviting people into their very ways of being and becoming—of defining what's normal, knowable, acceptable, or even desirable—then educators can question how and in whose best interest media messages are made. Recognizing the enabling and animating force of mass communication, instructors can facilitate conversations on how best to realize media that is good, just, virtuous, caring, and fair. Such discussions serve citizens, community members, and those otherwise requiring media literacy and ethical communication systems to live a quality life. Once we understand the sociological and cultural implications of media, then media ethics is for everyone.

Media ethics instructors can expand their conception of whom they serve—both media makers and citizens—while all media educators can embrace their role as ethics instructors. Because media is so vital in developing morally autonomous individuals and the process of democratic worldmaking, media educators can infuse ethical thinking into all pedagogy. To achieve this, media must not be seen as merely a transmitting of messages. Instead, it should be approached as an invitation to understand, approach, and be part of the world. Media education should consider the complete person—not just the part that sends or receives a message—and address people as active agents with a specific history, culture, and range of needs.

To help educators anticipate the direction of media and stay current with the ethical issues that arise, persist, and transform, this chapter offers a critical and care-based approach. Critical means recognizing communication as discursive, active, and contextual. This rigorous yet flexible outlook is then applied to the traditional concept of objectivity. This chapter concludes with some basic questions that media educators and citizen-users can ask going forward.

Today, the various types of media—as social institutions and cultural fields—continuously shift and work to (re)establish boundaries. Empowering citizens to be critical, caring, and media literate gives society the best chance to hold our life-defining communications accountable. Media educators can thus serve everyone, encouraging the conversations that are worth having and inviting the morally autonomous citizens necessary for widespread and free-flowing care.

## MEDIA ETHICS IS FOR EVERYONE

To understand where media ethics is going, it is important to know where media ethics has been. For a widely applicable analysis, it is useful to discern how media helps make people who they are. This is a material and discursive process, where the relational meaning-making of specific groups and the affordances of technology have measurable, empirical consequences and set the terms for being/becoming in the world. Using socially constructed communication and larger media systems, individuals meet their daily material needs and animate themselves into culturally specific manners of living. Our various languages do not reflect the world; they help to create it. Individuals are socialized by language into particular modes of organization and also use communication to shape and negotiate that social order. This process of making the world is *dialectical* and illuminates the ongoing importance of why cultivating ethical media practices is so vital to the formation of individuals and society.

In a dialectical (or critical) approach, reality does not consist of ready-made individuals, ideas, social institutions, or meanings. Instead, things and people exist in a dynamic process of development, a state of becoming defined by relationships, internal contradictions, external tensions, and the larger context of contingent circumstance. There is no such thing as an isolated, detached "individual," but neither is there an abstract and individual-less "society." Individual agents and larger social structures only exist because of each other, and in their entangled interaction, each cocreates the other. People, society, and things become what they are only in relation to one another. "One cannot be a self on one's own," and what we see as individual persons did not preexist their relationships or the cultures that helped form them.[3]

For humans, a key component of this ongoing dialectical development is language and communication. Today, this process increasingly involves the media. As they co-constitute particular ways of life and specific individuals, communication, and media are *discursive*. A discourse is a particular way of positioning, understanding, and talking about a topic or subject thus prioritizing certain practices, values, and truths. An active process, not a static thing, a discourse and its particular discursive practices of meaning-making develop over time in culturally specific ways.

People shape and are shaped by discourse. Active agents create a discourse that then invites them to approach life in a specific way, influencing how people treat, interact with, and construct their worlds. This discursive invitation, along with human agency and changing circumstances, results in people acting back and adjusting an order of discourse. The process then continues where discursive systems of meaning socialize specific kinds of individuals who then use their active agency to modify those systems.[4] A discourse is thus used by active agents and a specific order of discourse is continuously contested, maintained, reinforced, transformed, or surpassed. In terms of human society, discourse is shaped and constrained by social structures. It can help reproduce the social order, but it can also transform it. Discourse is a site of social contestation (and another reason media ethics are so crucial).[5] Discourse is not just a descriptive word for a language that reflects reality. It has material consequences and helps constitute and shape reality.

When it comes to social change and communication, we can analyze how a specific discourse is built over time, how its meanings and practices of creating meaning are accumulated, discarded, or transformed, and how this relates to our current context. We can observe the changing discursive practices or strategies used to create meaning and fix it into place. Symbols and the meanings they convey are contingent; they are so but not necessarily so. There is nothing inherent about carbon under pressure—a diamond—that equates it to romantic love and marriage, but there is a social history and discourse around marriage in certain cultures that fixes (or attempts to fix) the meaning of diamonds in place. While humans could live in endless ways and anything could mean anything, a discourse is a necessary limiting of meaning to make sense of the world. People are then enabled through this constraint, as they are directed toward specific priorities, values, and actions. A discourse, even as a closure of meaning and an attempt to fix a specific belief, is thus productive and guides people toward a particular way of living.[6]

Media ethics is for everyone, as media circulate various genres of discourse that necessarily fix meaning and invite us into our specific relationships with each other, ourselves, and the world. We negotiate and answer these invitations as active agents, using the meanings available to create our own positions and relatively fixed points of reality. What is traditionally seen as separate individuals sending and interpreting messages through various channels can now be approached as a dialectical, historical, and cumulative process of constant becoming where various discourses, individual agents, and social institutions mutually limit and co-constitute each other. Thinking sociologically and critically about how individuals, media, and society help make each other what they are means valuing the messages we exchange and ensuring they are ethically sound. Media ethics is not just for media makers, as citizens also have a vested interest in how they're invited into the world.

In this critical approach, all media instructors take responsibility for the power of media. They would intentionally include ethical concepts, scripts, and toolboxes for their students, or at least encourage thoughtful reflection and dialogue on the nature and quality of media. As the media are at least partially responsible for who we are and what we become, it is in everyone's best interest to cultivate good, just, and caring media.

## CARE-BASED COMMUNICATION

Media ethics is for everyone, but not everyone will have the same media ethics. Building on our critical—dialectical, discursive, and contingent—approach, we can use an ethics of care to anticipate ethical issues and the future of media. Like our critical approach, this is not to argue for an authoritative or universal definition of care ethics. Instead, care is offered as a rich assemblage of potential wisdom and a general orientation to think with and through ethical issues.

The words "care" and "curious" share a Latin root, and we can think of care ethics in communication as being attentive to and curious about the world. Like our critical view, a caring communication approach is particularly mindful of the relational and co-constituted nature of people and their worlds. Care ethics is also characterized by an attentiveness that is in the best interest of those who require care.[7] Individuals do not just project their own categories of understanding onto a situation or other people. Instead, caring communicators empathize and understand people on their own terms. This empathy does not mean caring communicators must agree with others or accept the terms of others. It simply means offering a competent and good faith attempt to understand the co-constituted and multifaceted specifics of a situation, context, or situated individual before judgment is passed and decisions are made.[8] Those decisions are based on the best interest of the cared-for and respects, as much as possible, their moral autonomy.[9]

All of us require care, but what care looks like depends on how specific people are embedded and co-constituted by their relationships, circumstances, and larger cultural context. Each of us also has unique and varying degrees of resources, power, and levels of vulnerability[10] to provide and receive care. Care ethics is not abstract and totalizing, asking only about universals like duty or utility; care ethics is specific and proportionate, also asking who or what needs care and how we can properly respond. Considering a full range of needs (and addressing the complete person) this approach appreciates how communication is built on fixing and excluding certain meanings. Caring communicators—even if they push back or disagree—thus center those in the margins or otherwise excluded.[11] This attentiveness is not an end in itself but a reflexive exercise to comprehensively notice and comprehend the diverse kinds of entangled worldmaking that nourish us. The purpose of such communication is to cultivate specific kinds of care, not to achieve some ideal social harmony, and is intended to give everyone their (and society its) best chance at reaching maximum potential.

Care ethics also reminds communicators that people are active human subjects with their own worlds, specifically situated in a social-discursive context, and not passive objects that simply receive messages. Traditional attempts at journalistic objectivity, for example, are thus inadequate to serve citizens' news needs. Offering a "just-the-facts," detached view fails to account for the selective narrowing of facts at the offset (i.e., agenda-setting), the interpretation of active audiences, and the discursive fixing of meaning and cultural assumptions of any given society. Strictly objective journalism thus confuses its limited and culturally determined viewpoint with a monopolized version of truth and reality. Without context or situating the truth about facts—in other words, without exploring how facts are made meaningful to active subjects—strict objectivity encourages confirmation bias and a mindless reproduction of the status quo.

In the 1890s, for example, when self-proclaimed fact-based newspapers like the *New York Times* reported violence against Black people, they would report objective facts like the location and names of people involved in a lynching. Such discursive practices, without context, assumed the guilt of the person lynched, and articles read as if an African American was simply getting what they supposedly deserved.[12] Enter Ida B. Wells, whose investigative reporting through interviewing accusers, questioning police, seeking witnesses, and gathering statistics was more critically attentive and did not just rely on official sources. Embedded in the community instead of abstractly removed, she found that many African Americans were lynched not for crimes, as was reported by newspapers, but because these particular Black folks showed signs of social success. The traditional press was limited by cultural biases, and "fact-based" reporting failed to uncover the truth about violence against Black Americans.[13] A supposed "view from nowhere" neutrality misinformed readers by reinforcing stereotypes and prejudice.[14] In other words, seemingly objective journalism reinforced the existing racial hierarchy and status quo. More subjective and marginalized (but no less true) views were thus epistemologically and morally necessary to counter hegemonic thinking and create more meaningful, caring, and comprehensively true forms of communication.

## CARING CRITICISM FOR QUALITY CONTROL

All communication has a point of view, and all media—no matter how neutral—is positioning the world and its audience in a specific way. To anticipate issues and stay current, all media instructors can view themselves as ethicists who serve citizens in the active process of constructing society and continually inviting individuals into who they are. Attentive and empathetic to how specific individuals are situated in society, embedded in their environments, entangled with other interests, and co-constituted by their relationships, media educators can ask whether their instruction is cultivating care. Are we addressing students as complete people and comprehensively meeting their needs? What about the needs of the citizens, systems, and nonhuman worlds that media makers will influence?

While the exact answers to these questions will vary for journalists, advertisers, video game designers, public relations specialists, and the various kinds of media being made, all media educators can ask whether specific communications are fulfilling their intended purpose of fostering community. This community is not defined as social harmony (as if different interests and values did not exist) but is instead a common world where people have the care and support to meet their potential. When reviewing lesson plans or evaluating specific issues, arguments, strategies, or media messages, we can ask whether the media is behaving in community-fostering ways on the left side of this table or the less-caring manner on the right.[15]

| Does specific media... | |
|---|---|
| Inform, interpret, analyze, explain | Misinform, assume, confuse, and stereotype |
| Investigate | Uncritically accept |
| Create worthwhile social conversations | Stifle, stop, or muddle social conversations |
| Generate empathy | Generate misunderstanding, hatred, and fear |
| Encourage accountability | Obfuscate and misdirect blame |

With more nuance, we can also continually question media through a critical lens and hold it accountable to the principles of care. When crafting a particular piece of media or evaluating specific media messages, we can thus ask the following questions. By answering these questions, we can gauge whether media takes responsibility for its co-constitutive nature, respects the moral autonomy of its users, and engenders the necessary attentiveness for a caring populace:

- How does the media message invite people to understand themselves, their world, and their place in it? How does it attempt to position people?
- How does the media message explain or obscure the relationships and co-constitutive nature of people, processes, institutions, nonhuman organisms, and things? Does it properly consider relationships, context, relative power, and levels of vulnerability?
- How does the media maker set meanings to interpret the world? What specific meaning(s) is the communication trying to fix in place? What is excluded? What are the particular consequences or implications of such meanings and exclusions for all manner of people?
- What cues do media makers provide for interpretation; what do they presuppose as true? Are these presuppositions fair? Do they respect the moral autonomy and dignity of citizen-audiences and those represented in the discourse?
- What argument is the media message making? What is it trying to do? Does it do so in a way that is fair to the vulnerable? Whose needs are and are not being met?

- How does the media message invite individuals into their identity and regulate social belonging by defining what is normal and desirable? How does this align with or challenge the helpful/harmful aspects of the status quo?

This list is not exhaustive, but it can help us understand how ethics can apply to every type of media. All communication is an act of worldmaking, and we can all help build better, more caring worlds.

**NOTES**

1. James W. Carey, *Communication as Culture: Essays on Media and Society* (New York: Routledge, 1988), 1–33.

2. John Durham Peters, *Speaking into the Air: A History of the Idea of Communication* (University of Chicago Press, 1999).

3. Charles Taylor, *Sources of the Self: The Making of the Modern Identity* (Cambridge: Cambridge University Press, 1989), 36; Donna Haraway, *When Species Meet* (Minneapolis: University of Minnesota Press, 2008); Sandra Harding, "Rethinking Standpoint Epistemology: What is 'Strong Objectivity,'" *Centennial Review* 36, no. 3 (Fall 1992): 437–70.

4. Norman Fairclough, *Language and Power*, 3rd edition (New York: Routledge, 2015).

5. Norman Fairclough, *Discourse and Social Change* (Malden: Blackwell, 1992), 10–16.

6. See, for example, Teun A. van Dijk, "Discourse as Interaction in Society," in *Discourse as Social Interaction*, edited by Teun A. van Dijk (New York: Sage, 1997), 1–37; Theo van Leeuwen, *Discourse and Practice: New Tools for Critical Discourse Analysis* (New York: Oxford University Press, 2008).

7. Nel Noddings, *Caring: A Feminine Approach to Ethics and Moral Education* (Berkeley: University of California Press, 1984), 11–71.

8. Joseph P. Jones, "Caring with the Public: An Integration of Feminist Moral, Environmental, and Political Philosophy in Journalism Ethics," *Journal of Media Ethics* 36, no. 2 (2021): 74–84.

9. Grace Clement, *Care, Autonomy, and Justice: Feminism and the Ethic of Care* (New York: Routledge, 1996).

10. Vulnerability is defined here as a lack of resources and power.

11. bell hooks, *Feminist Theory: From Margin to Center*, 2nd edition (New York: South End Press, 2000).

12. "Lynching in Georgia," *New York Times*, September 16, 1897.

13. David T. Z. Mindich, *Just the Facts: How "Objectivity" Came to Define American Journalism* (New York University Press, 1998), 113–37.

14. Lewis Raven Wallace, *The View from Somewhere: Undoing the Myth of Journalistic Objectivity* (University of Chicago Press, 2019).

15. The left side of this table is derived from the journalistic roles for society in Stephanie Craft and Charles N. Davis, *Principles of American Journalism: An Introduction*, 2nd edition (New York: Routledge, 2016), 1–30. While these social roles originated in journalism studies, they can apply to all forms of media.

# Index

abilities, public relations ethics and, 86–88
abstracts, 125–126
access, and sports reporting, 120–121
accessibility, 49–50
Accrediting Council for Education in Journalism and Mass Communication (AEJMC), vii–viii, 58
accuracy, 65–67, 69, 114
advanced courses: public relations ethics, 83–90; undergraduate media ethics, 19–25
Africa, coverage of, 152
agency: and discourse, 169; gender and, 152
Anscome, Elizabeth, 5
applied ethics, 4; public relations ethics and, 84–85; Thomas on, 28–29
Arbery, Ahmaud, 96
argumentation, Thomas on, 31
Aristotle, 3, 5, 23, 132
artificial intelligence, 67, 123, 125
Asia, coverage of, 152
assessments: alternate, 47–48; public relations ethics and, 87

assignments: on civic journalism, 158, 160, 162, 164; on digital ethics, 125–126; diversity and, 39–40, 42; graduate-level, 31; inclusivity and, 48; on law/ethics, 61–62; on mental health/suicide, 137; problem-based, 21–23; on public relations ethics, 86–87; for reporting course, 66–67, 69–70; on science communication ethics, 145–147; undergraduate-level, 16–17
Associated Press, 70, 111, 136, 141
Association of American Universities Committee on Graduate Education, 29
audience: civic journalism and, 157–165; ethics for, 78
Augustine, saint, 5
authority, deference to, 110
autonomy, 15
Azoulay, Ariella, 78–79

Baerbock, Charlotte Alma, 139–140
beginning activities: Newton on, 124; Wilkins on, 66–70
beneficence, 3
Bentham, Jeremy, 6

175

Bergen, Lori, 129–133
bias: and data ethics, 113–118; and foreign reporting, 151–152; Jones on, 172
biosafety, 143–144
BIPOC communities: civic journalism and, 159; coverage and, 172
bird flu, 143–144
Bobkowski, Piotr, 41
Bodinger-de Uriarte, Cristine, 40
Bok, Sissela, 85
boundaries, media and, 168
Bovée, Warren, 28–29
Breslin, Jack, 55–63
broadcast news classes, 91–97
Brunner, B. R., 87

Callahan, Daniel, 28
care: for context, 94–96; ethics of, 7, 132, 168, 170–172; in interviews, 92; term, 171
Carter, Kevin, 78
case analyses, 86–87
case briefs, 62
case studies, 13–14; assignments on, 16–17; Breslin on, 57; for law/ethics course, 61–62; for public relations ethics, 86–87; for reporting course, 72; resources for, 14; Thomas on, 28; on unpublishing, 111
categorical imperative, 6
Chauvin, Derek, 109
citizen engagement: law/ethics course on, 60; relational journalism and, 130, 132
civic journalism, 157–165; backlash to, 160; definition of, 157; recommendations for, 162–164
class discussions: critical, 31; public relations ethics and, 86; in reporting course, 66; Scott on, 76–77
codes of ethics: public relations ethics and, 85, 87; Society of Professional Journalists, 92, 101; standalone courses and, 83; student-developed, 31, 59, 126, 137
Coles, Robert, 41

collaboration, civic journalism and, 157–165
collective learning, relational journalism and, 130
Columbus, Christopher, 95
combined courses: issues with, 55–57; media law/ethics, 55–63; public relations ethics, 83–84
Commission on Public Relations Education (CPRE), 83
commitment: civic journalism and, 158–160; relational journalism and, 130–131
communitarianism, 7
community, 15–16, 169, 173; civic journalism and, 157–165; relational journalism and, 129–133; reporting and, 70; student journalism and, 101, 104–105; term, 167
community conversation, 24
conflicts of interest, student journalism and, 101–103
Confucianism, 7, 132
consequentialist ethics, 6–7
content moderation laws, 140–141
context issues, 94–96
conventional representation, 77–79
copyright issues, 93–94
coverage audit, 112
Craig, David A., 139, 141
creative exercises, on digital ethics, 125
credit, for videos, 94
criminal justice issues, reporting on, 109–112
Crisis Text Line, 115–116
critical thinking, 168–170, 172; and data ethics, 116; law/ethics course and, 58–59, 61; and social media, 161–162
cultural ethics, public relations ethics and, 85–86
Culver, Kathleen Bartzen, vii–ix, 109–112, 135–138
current issues, law/ethics course on, 59
curriculum, diversifying, 37–44

data, term, 113–114
data ethics, 113–118
Dayton Serves, 40
debate: Scott on, 76–77. *See also* class discussions
decision-making models: Navigation Wheel, 150; public relations ethics and, 85
deference to authority, 110
de Middel, Cristina, 77
democracy: AAU on, 29; relational journalism and, 131–132
deontology, 5–6, 84
Deuze, Mark, 123
dialectic, 169
digital ethics, 123–127; definitional issues with, 123; issues in, 125; versus social media, 140
dignity, student journalism and, 104
Dimensions of Difference Guide, 160–161
discourse, 169–170
distributive justice, 6
diversity: civic journalism and, 159; and class discussions, 31–32; and coverage, 172; and ethics curriculum, 37–44; need for, 20–22; public relations ethics and, 85–86, 88; relational journalism and, 131; and survey approach, 79; and visual ethics, 76
Drew, Richard, 78
duty ethics, 5–6

Ellis, Paula Lynn, 129–133
engagement: civic journalism and, 157–165; with ethical questions, 57, 78–79; public relations ethics and, 86; Scott on, 76–77; with social problems, 38. *See also* citizen engagement
environmental journalism, 143–148
episodic coverage, 111–112
epistemology, feminist standpoint, 7–8
ethics: definition of, 3–4, 124; prinicples in, 14–16; of process versus meaning, 75–76; Stewart on, vii
ethics instruction: Breslin on, 60–61; goals of, 28–29; importance of, vii–ix; Poepsel on, 158–164
exams, public relations ethics and, 87
expectations, and introductory reporting courses, 65
experiential learning, 23–24; diversity and, 42
extractive journalism, 130
eye contact, 68

fabrication, 100
Facebook, 115
fairness, and data use, 115
fair use issues, 93–94
fandom, and sports reporting, 119–120
fault lines approach, 38–39
Fazio, Lisa, 95
feminist ethical theories, 7–8
films: ethics assignments on, 22; law/ethics course and, 61; portrayals of journalists in, 13; reporting course and, 68–70
Finneman, Teri, 41
First Amendment education, Breslin on, 58
Floyd, George, 93, 96, 99, 109
foreign correspondence, 149–153
Fouchier, Ron, 143–144
framing, science communication and, 143–146; assignment on, 147
Frare, Therese, 79
Frazier, Darnella, 93
freebies, and sports reporting, 120–121
future: focus on, 46; of media ethics, 167–168, 171

Gardner, Howard, 48
gender: and coverage, 152; and ethical theories, 7–8
genetically modified organisms (GMOs), 145
global ethics, public relations ethics and, 85–86
Golden Mean, 132

good, nature of, 3–4
*The Good Place*, 13
government sources, and accuracy, 114
graduate education, 27–35; foreign correspondence, 149–153; goals of, 29
Grazado, Emma, 92
Greenpeace, 145

harassment, online, 141
Hariman, Robert, 78
harm, 15, 45–46; broadcast journalism and, 92–93; reporting and, 70–71
health issues: journalism and, 143–148; mental health as, 135–136
Hendricks, Marina, 41
Hickerson, C. A., 87
Holliman, Richard, 144

images: areas of ethical concern with, 74; digital ethics and, 123; ontology of, 79. *See also* photography
inclusion: civic journalism and, 159; ethics instruction and, 45–52; public relations ethics and, 85–86, 88; relational journalism and, 131
influence, civic journalism and, 157–165
information collection, from human sources, 67–68
informed consent: and interviews, 92; and student journalism, 103
intersectionality, Maynard fault lines approach and, 38–39
interviews: guidelines for, 92; initial, 66; in-person, 67–68; transparency in, 68–69
introductory reporting courses, 65–72

Johns Hopkins, 137
Johnson, Patrick R., 19–25, 45–52
Jones, Joseph, 167–174
justice issues, 109–112

Kant, Immanuel, 6
Karlov, Andrei, 78

Kirby, David, 79
knowledge, public relations ethics and, 84–86, 88
Kobre, Ken, 75
Kolber, Suzy, 93
Kraft, Nicole, vii–ix, 99–106, 119–122
Kurdi, Alan, 39, 78
Kvalnes, Øyvind, 150

Lalwani, Sheila B., 139–142, 149–153
language: and society, 169; on suicide, 136
Latin America, coverage of, 152
law/ethics course, 55–63; convergence/conflict in, 60; importance of, 57–58
learning outcomes: on diversity, 37–38; for law/ethics course, 58–60
legal issues, reporting on, 109–112
Lester, Paul, 74
LGTBQIA+ issues, coverage of, 152
listening post assignment, 41–42
Littler, Ed, 120
local issues. *See* community
long-term effects: broadcasting and, 91; of naming, 110–111; relational journalism and, 130–131; student publications and, 103
loyalty, and sports reporting, 119–120
Lucaites, J. L., 78

The Marshall Project, 112
May, Todd, 13
Maynard, Robert, 38
McCurry, Steve, 77
McDowell, Michael, 20
McLuhan, Marshall and Eric, 126
McNealy, Jasmine E., 113–118
meaning, ethics of, 75–76
media, definition of, 2
media analysis, assignments on, 17, 22
media ethics: definition of, 1–8; importance of, 167–174; recommendations for, 172–174
media literacy, 11–12
mental health issues, 135–138

metaethics: frameworks in, 4–8; nature of, 3; tenets of, 12
Mill, John Stuart, 6, 132
misinformation, 125; context and, 94–96; reporting courses on, 67; social media and, 139–142
misogyny, 139–141
Moeller, Susan, 151
moral assertion, versus ethical deliberation, 3–4
Moral Machine experiment, 12
moral philosophy, 1, 3–4; *The Good Place* on, 13; public relations ethics and, 84
multiple intelligences, 47–48

Namath, Joe, 93
naming, 110–111
Navigation Wheel, 150
Neher, William W., 30, 32
new media, law/ethics course on, 59
news aggregators, 11
newsrooms: and diversity, 40–41; experiences in, and ethics, 100
Newton, April, 91–97
Njewton, Julianne H., 123–127
normative claims, 3
NPR, 92, 141
Nyhan, Brendan, 95

objectivity: civic journalism and, 161; Jones on, 171–172; relational journalism and, 131; and sports reporting, 119–120
on-the-record, 69, 92
ontology, 123

Page (Arthur W.) Center, 85–87
Painter, Chad, 30, 37–44, 87
parachute journalism, 151
partnerships, diversity and, 40–41
Patterson, Philip, 30, 87
photography: ethics and, 39, 73–81; out of context, 95. *See also* images
phronesis, 5
Place, Katie R., 83–90
plagiarism, 100

Plaisance, Patrick Lee, 1–8, 11–17, 30
Plato, 5
Poepsel, Mark, 157–165
police, media ethics and, 70–71, 109–110, 172
politics, social media and, 139–141
popular culture, and media ethics, 13
position papers: and diversity, 39–40; for law/ethics course, 62. *See also* written assignments
Potter, Ralph B., Jr., 85
Potter Box, 38–39, 85
PowerPoint, 60–61
privacy, 15–16; social media and, 141; student journalism and, 103; visuals and, 75
problem solving, relational journalism and, 129–130
process, ethics of, 75–76
professionals, ethics for, 32–33
project-based learning, 20–23
Project CRISS, 50
proper distance, 78
public journalism, 157–165
public relations, versus civic journalism, 158
public relations ethics course, 83–90; recommendations for, 88–89
Public Relations Society of America (PRSA), 85, 87
Pyle, Ernie, 150–151

quotes, cleaning up, 69

Radio Television Digital News Association, 96
rapport, 68
Rawls, John, 6–7, 132
Reality Checklist, for civic journalism, 158
reasoning: Thomas on, 31. *See also* critical thinking
red flags, law/ethics course on, 59
reflection, 45, 50–51; in experiential learning, 23; one-minute essay, 79; public relations ethics and, 87–88; Scott on, 76–77

relational journalism, 129–133
relationship-building: sports reporting and, 120–121; student journalism and, 101
ren, 7
reporting courses: foreign correspondence, 149–153; introductory, 65–72; law and justice issues in, 65–72; sports, 119–122
representations, 47; conventional, 77–79
resilience, ethics instruction and, 24–25
resources, 43; for case studies, 14, 87, 111; for mental health, 136–137; for reporting ethics, 72; for undergraduate ethics instruction, 27n1–3
respect, student journalism and, 104
responsibility, 15; of spectatorship, 78
retractions, 71
Ross, W. D., 6
Russo, Eve (Tannery), 91–93

Samaha, Joel, 61
science communication, 143–148; triangle of, 143–144
Scott, Alex, 73–81
Seech, Zachary, 31
self-reflection. *See* reflection
service learning, 41–42
silence, versus coverage, as ethical issue, 96
skills, public relations ethics and, 86–88
social justice, ethics instruction and, 25
social media, 139–142; and broadcast journalism, 91; and civic journalism, 161–162; definition of, 139; and photography ethics, 73; and representation, 77–78
Society of Professional Journalists Code of Ethics, 92, 101
Socrates, 5
Socratic instruction, 13, 61
Solutions Journalism Network, 130, 136
sources: and accuracy, 114; compensating, 94; harm to, reducing, 92–93; multiple, 69–70; reporting courses and, 67–68; student journalism and, 103–104; threats from, 71
spectatorship, responsibility of, 78
sports reporting, 119–122
*Spotlight*, 40, 68, 70
standpoint epistemology, feminist, 7–8
Stanford University Library, 93–94
Steen, Rob, 120
stereotypes: and foreign reporting, 151–152; Scott on, 77–79
Stewart, Potter, vii
Stim, Richard, 94
Stony Brook Center for News Literacy, 94–95
story exercise, personal ethics-related, 126
student media: civic journalism and, 160–161; diversity and, 42; ethics in, 99–106; reporting course and, 71; sports reporting and, 120
style rules, and ethical issues, 70–71
suffering. *See* ugly news; victims
suicide, 135–138
Sullenberger, Chesley, 93
support, professional, 163–164
Supreme Court, law/ethics course on, 59
survey approach, Scott on, 74, 78–79
syllabus: accessibility and, 49–50; Johnson on, 46
Systematic Ethical Analysis, 75

TARES test, 85
teacher preparation, inclusion and, 45–52
technology, access to, 50
thematic coverage, 111–112
theoretical ethics, 4
theory, on ethics, 4–8, 12–13; Breslin on, 57; Newton on, 124; Scott on, 75; Thomas on, 28, 32
Thérèse of Lisieux, saint, 41
Thomas, Ryan J., 27–35
threats, from sources, 71
Till, Emmett, 79

transparency, 16; civic journalism and, 160; and conflicts of interest, 102; and data use, 115–116; relational journalism and, 129; reporting courses and, 68–69
trust: civic journalism and, 158, 160; foreign correspondents and, 150; and outside-newsroom materials, 94; relational journalism and, 129; reporting and, 68; science communication and, 144–145
truth, in reporting, 66–67, 69

*ubuntu*, 7
Ugland, Erick, 58
ugly news: coverage of, 135–138; ethical issues and, 96; student journalism and, 104
undergraduate media ethics, 11–17; advanced, 19–25
Universal Design for Learning, 49
University of Texas Center for Media Engagement, 111
University of Wisconsin-Madison Center for Journalism Ethics, 111
unpublishing, 110–111; requests for, 103–104
useful knowledge, 78
Ut, Nick, 78
utilitarianism, 6, 132

vaccines, coverage of, 144
Valgeirsson, Gunnar, 40
veil of ignorance, 6–7
victims, coverage of, 135–138; broadcast journalism and, 91–93; gender and, 152; interview guidelines for, 92; naming and, 110–111; visuals and, 75, 78–79
video, from outside newsroom, 93–94
virtue ethics, 5
visual ethics, 73–81; issues in, 74–76
Voakes, Paul S., 129–133
voice(s): in debate, 76–77; diversifying, 47

Ward, Stephen, 124, 140
Wells, Ida B., 172
Wilkins, Lee, 30, 65–72, 87
work-life balance, 163
World Health Organization (WHO), 144
written assignments: on digital ethics, 125–126; graduate-level, 31; issues with, 47–48; for law/ethics course, 61–62; prompts for, diversity in, 40. *See also* position papers

Yahr, Natalie, 92

Zhang, Xiaochen Angela, 83–90
Zlaten, Rhema, 143–148

# About the Contributors

**Lori Bergen** is the founding dean of the College of Media, Communication and Information at the University of Colorado Boulder, where she holds the James E. de Castro Chair in Global Media Studies. As leader of CU Boulder's first new college in more than 50 years, Bergen's focus is on the interdisciplinary approach to media, communication, and information education. Bergen came to Colorado from Marquette University, where she was dean of the Diederich College of Communication and the Burleigh and Scripps Professor. Bergen is coauthor of *Media Violence and Aggression: Science and Ideology* and *News for US: Citizen-Centered Journalism*.

After earning his doctorate at the University of Minnesota, **Jack Breslin** has been teaching a combined media law and ethics class at Iona University for 22 years. Prior to his academic career, he enjoyed two decades as a journalist and network TV publicist with NBC and FOX.

**Kathleen Bartzen Culver** is the James E. Burgess Chair in Journalism Ethics, director of the University of Wisconsin–Madison School of Journalism and Mass Communication, and director of the Center for Journalism Ethics. Long interested in the implications of digital media on journalism and public interest communication, Culver integrates research, teaching, and service to advance integrity in media. She also studies free expression, especially in campus contexts. She serves as visiting faculty for the Poynter Institute for Media Studies and was the founding editor of PBS MediaShift's education section.

## About the Contributors

**Paula Lynn Ellis** has long been a leader in journalism innovation, transformative change, and community engagement. She worked for Knight Ridder for 26 years, as a reporter, editor, managing editor, publisher, and corporate vice president for operations. In 2006, she became vice president for strategic initiatives at Knight Foundation, where she led transformative change efforts in journalism and communities, national grantmaking, and evaluation. Ellis is a senior associate at the Kettering Foundation, trustee of the Poynter Institute, and a director of the National Conference on Citizenship. She is a coauthor of *News for US: Citizen-Centered Journalism*.

**Patrick R. Johnson** MJE, is an assistant professor of journalism and the director of Student Media in the Diederich College of Communication at Marquette University. He studies the intersection of news literacy, journalism practice, and journalism education to create more equitable and sustainable futures for journalism and its audiences. He also focuses on LGBTQIA+ media, issues, and knowledge production in his research. In teaching, Johnson is most often in an ethics classroom and identifying ways to improve all JMC pedagogy. Johnson is a research affiliate of Trusting News, where he works to find ways to bridge trust-gaps between audiences and journalists.

**Joseph Jones** is assistant professor at the Reed College of Media at West Virginia University. He specializes in media history, ethics, sociology, political economy, and critical theory. His research includes the history of the Black press, the need for feminist theory in journalism studies, and the ethical obligations of lifestyle journalists. Joe earned his PhD in 2021 from the Missouri School of Journalism, and in 2022 won the Penn State Davis Ethics Award for his dissertation on incorporating care ethics into food journalism. Overall, he asks how media can help invite us to be the best version of ourselves.

**Nicole Kraft** is associate professor of journalism practice at The Ohio State University, where she teaches media writing and editing, sports journalism, sports media relations, feature writing, and media law and ethics. She is also the director of Ohio State's Sports and Society Initiative and author of *Always Get the Name of the Dog: A Guide to Media Interviewing* and the open-educational textbook *Writing Fabulous Features*. Nicole is an award-winning news and magazine journalist and designer, and former congressional press secretary. She also served in communication roles in the NBA and in the wine industry, and currently covers the NHL's Columbus Blue Jackets for the Associated Press and horse racing for the *Columbus Dispatch*.

**Sheila B. Lalwani** is a doctoral student at the Moody College of Communication at the University of Texas at Austin. As a research associate at the Technology Information and Policy Institute at the University of Texas at Austin, her research focuses on international media, information law, and policy in the United States and the European Union. She is also a cyber fellow at the Strauss Center for International Security and Law. She was awarded a Fulbright scholarship to Germany and holds an LLM in legal theory from Goethe University and a master's in public policy from Harvard University.

**Jasmine E. McNealy** is an internationally recognized scholar whose research is interdisciplinary, centered at the intersection of media, technology, policy, and law. Of particular focus are the areas of privacy, surveillance, and data governance and the impacts on marginalized and vulnerable communities. Her research has been published in social science, law, ethics, and computer science journals. Public institutions, private foundations, and private organizations have funded her research.

**April Newton** is journalism teaching faculty at Loyola University Maryland and a PhD candidate at the University of Maryland. April teaches journalism skills courses as well as media ethics, documentary history, and documentary production at the undergraduate level and emerging media ethics and media innovation at the graduate level. April's research focuses on the experiences of women working in journalism and her teaching priorities are to empower students to develop confidence in their growing skills while incorporating diversity and inclusion into every class to help develop more effective journalists and curious adults with an interest in changing their world for the better.

**Julianne H. Newton** is the director of the communication and media studies doctoral and master's program and professor of visual communication at the School of Journalism and Communication at the University of Oregon. An award-winning scholar and educator, she has worked as a reporter, editor, photographer, and designer for newspapers, magazines, electronic media, and organizations. Her research applies ethics and cognitive theory to the study of visual behavior, focusing on journalism and media. She teaches courses on digital ethics, research methods, visual theory, and media and society.

**Chad Painter** is department chair and an associate professor of communication at the University of Dayton, where he teaches courses in journalism and mass communication. He earned a doctorate from the University of Missouri School of Journalism. He studies media ethics with an emphasis on the depiction of journalists in popular culture, the alternative press, and diversity studies. He coauthored *Media Ethics: Issues and Cases* and *Entertaining Ethics: Lessons in Media Ethics from Popular Culture*. He has eight years of professional experience as a reporter, editor, and public relations practitioner for print and online publications.

**Patrick Lee Plaisance** is the Don W. Davis Professor in Ethics at the Bellisario College of Communications at Penn State University. His research focuses on media ethics theory, moral psychology theory, and applications of the philosophy of technology to media practice. He is the editor of the *Journal of Media Ethics*. He is the author of *Media Ethics: Key Principles for Responsible Practice* and *Virtue in Media: The Moral Psychology of Excellence in News and Public Relations*. He edited *Communication and Media Ethics* (volume 26 in the *Handbooks of Communication Science* series) and has published two dozen journal articles.

**Katie R. Place** is professor of public relations at Quinnipiac University whose research examines the nexus of power, ethics, and listening in public relations. She has authored more than 60 conference papers or publications in such peer-reviewed journals as the *Journal of Public Relations Research, Public Relations Review, Journal of Mass Media Ethics,* and *Journal of Communication Management*. She is the past head of the Public Relations Division of AEJMC and resides on the editorial boards of the *Journal of Public Relations Research, Journal of Media Ethics, Journal of Public Relations Education,* and *Journal of Public Interest Communications*.

**Mark Poepsel** is associate professor of mass communication at Southern Illinois University–Edwardsville. His research interests include threats against journalists and engagement journalism. Poepsel teaches media entrepreneurship, science and media literacy, publication design, advanced broadcast writing, introductory mass communication theory, introductory media writing, and graduate research methods. He was recently awarded a grant from the Department of Education through the Consortium of Academic and Research Libraries in Illinois to develop the open-educational resource textbook, *The OER Guide to Media Writing*.

**Alex Scott** is assistant professor of multimedia storytelling in the School of Journalism and Mass Communication at the University of Iowa. His research examines the routines of photojournalism and the construction of social differences in nonfiction visuals. He previously worked as a photojournalist and a photo editor for various news outlets in New York before completing his PhD at the University of Texas at Austin.

**Ryan J. Thomas** is associate professor of journalism and media production and the director of graduate studies in the Edward R. Murrow College of Communication at Washington State University. His research on media ethics amid processes of change has been published in such journals as the *Journal of Media Ethics, Journalism Studies,* and *Digital Journalism*. He has taught classes on media ethics, journalism and democracy, the sociology of news, and qualitative research methods.

**Paul S. Voakes** is professor emeritus at the College of Media, Communication and Information at the University of Colorado Boulder. Voakes served on the faculty of the School of Journalism at Indiana University from 1994 to 2003, when he became dean of the School of Journalism and Mass Communication at Colorado. He is a coauthor of *The American Journalist in the 21st Century, Working with Numbers and Statistics,* and, most recently, *News for US: Citizen-Centered Journalism*. Before becoming an educator, Voakes was a newspaper journalist in the San Francisco Bay Area for 15 years.

**Lee Wilkins** is professor emerita from the School of Journalism at the University of Missouri, where she taught ethics for more than 20 years and received school, campus, and university-system awards for teaching. Her research focuses on the moral development of professional journalists and the applications of neuroscience to ethical decision-making. She is the coauthor of the text *Media Ethics: Issues and Cases* (now in its 11th edition); *Entertaining Ethics*, which tracks media ethics issues as explored in popular film, television, and music; and *The Moral Media*, an exploration of professional moral development. She is a member of the founding editorial board of the *Journal of Media Ethics* and was editor of that publication for six years.

**Xiaochen Angela Zhang** is assistant professor in public relations at the Gaylord College of Journalism and Mass Communication at the University of Oklahoma. Her research focuses on crisis and risk communication, digital media strategic communication, and ethics. She teaches ethics in public relations and strategic communication at both undergraduate and graduate levels.

**Rhema Zlaten** is assistant professor of mass communication at Colorado Mesa University. She researches the future of digital journalism, science communication, autonomy in media work, and rhetoric in the news. Her professional background is in print and digital journalism, both as a full-time journalist and as a freelance writer. She integrates media ethics into each of her classes, ranging from freshmen media history classes to senior-level advanced journalism, opinion writing, and arts journalism classes.

www.ingramcontent.com/pod-product-compliance
Lightning Source LLC
Chambersburg PA
CBHW030121240426
43673CB00041B/1359